101 DEFENSIVE FOOTBALL DRILLS

VOLUME 1:

INDIVIDUAL SKILL DRILLS

Bill Arnsparger
James A. Peterson

ISBN: 1-58518-299-0
Library of Congress Catalog Card Number: 00-1042239

Book layout and diagrams: Jennifer Bokelmann
Cover design: Jennifer Bokelmann
Front cover photo: David Stanley

Coaches Choice
P.O. Box 1828
Monterey, CA 93942
www.coacheschoice.com

To the players and coaches that were my associates during my career that helped to make this book possible.

-Bill Arnsparger

ACKNOWLEDGMENTS

Any undertaking the size of this one reaches completion only through the cooperation of many people. To all of those to whom we are indebted, we say a heartfelt thank you. However, there were some among that group whose contributions require special notice; to Jim Peterson, my co-author, and his wife, Sue; to my wife, Betty Jane, and our daughter, Mary Susan, for providing me with encouragement; and to our son, David, for his suggestions and overall contributions. To all of these people, we offer our sincere gratitude. We couldn't have done it without you.

Bill Arnsparger

CONTENTS

PART I: MOVEMENT DRILLS

Chapter

PART II: SKILL DRILLS

Football drills are like medicine. The proper prescription can help a team in innumerable ways. The coach, however, has the ultimate responsibility to administer the "medicine" at the right time, in the right amount, and in the right way.

In that regard, all drills should be conducted in a learning atmosphere where every player is given every opportunity to be successful. When an athlete does well, he should be praised. When an athlete's performance does not measure up to expectations, he should be given constructive feedback that enables him to redirect his efforts in such a manner to achieve the desired change.

The technique or skill being stressed in a particular drill should be *over emphasized.* Coaches should insist and strive for perfection in every drill, by every player, on every repetition.

While many drills typically include specific pieces of equipment (e.g., blocking dummies), coaches should keep in mind that all drills could just as easily be conducted with players used as replacements for any recommended equipment. The one relatively indispensable piece of equipment is a regulation football. Whenever possible, a football should be incorporated into the drill and the offensive cadence should be simulated.

Finally, in my almost five decades of coaching, I have come to recognize and appreciate the capacity of properly conducted drills to serve as positive coaching tools. In the process, I have attempted to identify what factors seem to have the most meaningful impact on the extent to which a particular drill achieves its intended goals. To that end, I believe that every coach should adhere to the following eight drill axioms:

1. *Facilitate success:* When using a drill to teach a specific skill, care and patience must be taken by the coach to insure that the player is successful in the drill. All factors considered, we learn quicker when we are successful.

2. *Controlled situation:* If it is an <u>offensive drill,</u> the defensive man must give resistance but allow the offensive player to be successful. If it is a <u>defensive drill,</u> the offensive man must give resistance but allow the defensive player to be successful. This factor is very important in teaching tackling and blocking.

3. *Football and cadence:* Whatever the general focus of the drill—offensive or defensive—a regulation football should be used and a cadence simulated. This step stresses from the beginning the importance of:

   • Offensively, we must move on the cadence. At times on offense—even in a noisy stadium, the offense must move on the ball.

   • Defensively, we must move on the movement of the ball.

4. *Step-by-step teaching:* The Coach must have knowledge of the technique or fundamental that is being taught by the drill. The Coach must be able to demonstrate the technique or fundamental being taught. If the Coach is unable to perform the required skills, another player that is proficient in the technique or fundamental should be used to demonstrate the action. The technique or fundamental should be broken down in parts. This approach is called step-by-step teaching and is a major key to learning quickly.

5. *Be selective:* Pick out a few drills that will teach and simulate the technique or fundamental that is intended to be taught. While variation is needed, the Coach should remember that every player must always know the purpose of the drill and know the technique or fundamental that is being practiced.

6. *Emphasize the point:* The technique or fundamental being taught in a drill should always be exaggerated. This step is most easily accomplished in a controlled situation.

7. *Teamwork:* The individual drill is where TEAMWORK begins. First, listen to the instructions. Second, if a verbal signal is used, listen for the command. Third, work for perfection.

8. *Team success:* Individual drills to improve player skills are necessary to TEAM success. Make sure the player understands the drill, why it is necessary, and then create a learning situation for him to be successful.

CHAPTER 1

WARM-UP DRILLS

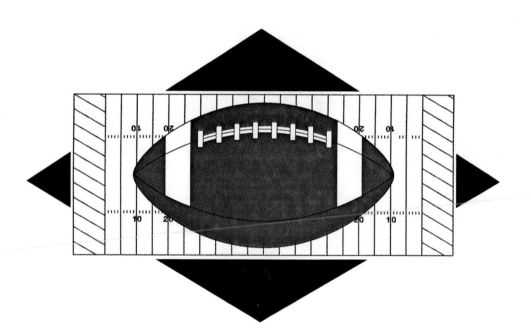

DRILL #1: HIGH KNEE

Objective: To warm-up.

Equipment Needed: None.

Description: On the coach's command, the player runs in place. Special emphasis is placed on having the player lift his knees at least as high as his waist. He should hold his arms at a 90-degree angle, keeping his elbows bent. The high knee drill should be run in three stages. The player should start slowly and gradually build to a faster pace, then slow down. When the player enters the third stage and begins to slow his feet, he should concentrate on lifting his knees and maintaining his balance.

Coaching Points:

- Variety can be added to the drill by having the player run forward or backward at various speeds.

- The player should stay on the balls of his feet—not the heels or toes.

- The player can loosen his shoulders by swinging his arms in a full circle as he runs in place.

- The coach's command should be visual or verbal.

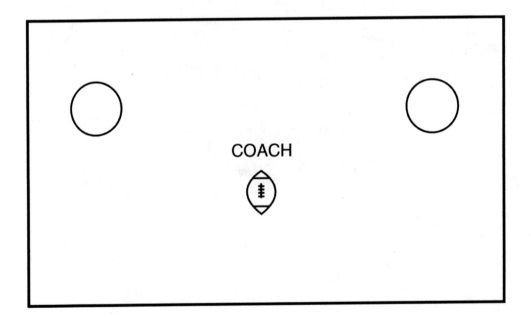

DRILL #2: HIGH KNEE CROSS-OVER

Objective: To warm-up.

Equipment Needed: None.

Description: The player straddles a chalk line. On the coach's command, the player runs forward down the chalk line. Special emphasis is placed on having the player lift his knees at least as high as his waist. He should alternately step on the opposite side of the chalk line as he moves forward. He should keep his elbows bent and his hands relaxed as he pumps his arms.

Coaching Points:

- Special emphasis should be placed on having the player keep his head up as he runs down the line.

- The player should not lean backward as he runs down the line.

- The player should keep his elbows close to his body as he runs down the line.

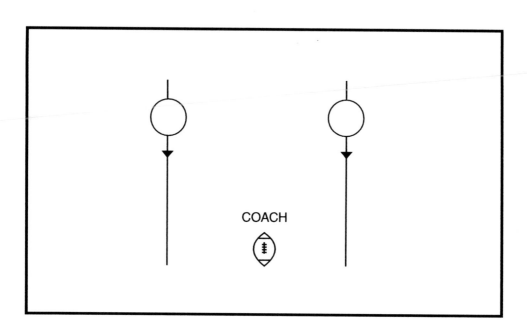

DRILL #3: SLOW-CARIOCCA

Objective: To warm-up.

Equipment Needed: None.

Description: The player assumes the ready position (i.e., his feet are placed no wider than his shoulders; his knees are bent and over his feet; his weight is evenly distributed over his feet; he has a slight bend at the waist; his head is up; his elbows are bent with his arms extended). On the coach's command, the player moves sideways, alternately placing one foot in front and one foot in back. In the slow-cariocca drill, the player should exaggerate the length of his stride. The player should move in a slow moving pace similar to a slow walk.

Coaching Points:

- The player should keep his hips flexed.

- The player should pull his shoulders back and keep his lower back arched, so that his back is flat.

- The coach should emphasize that each player maintain a proper ready position.

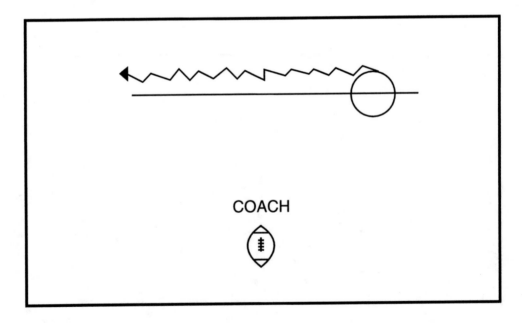

COACH

DRILL #4: QUICK-CARIOCCA

Objective: To warm-up.

Equipment Needed: None.

Description: The player assumes the ready position. On the coach's command, the player moves sideways, alternately placing one foot in front and one foot in back. In the quick-cariocca drill, the player should take extremely small steps. While moving his feet quickly, the player should attempt to take as many cariocca steps as possible in a five-yard distance.

Coaching Points:

- The player should keep his hips flexed.

- The player should pull his shoulders back and keep his lower back arched, so that his back is flat.

- The player should not hurry to cover the five-yard distance.

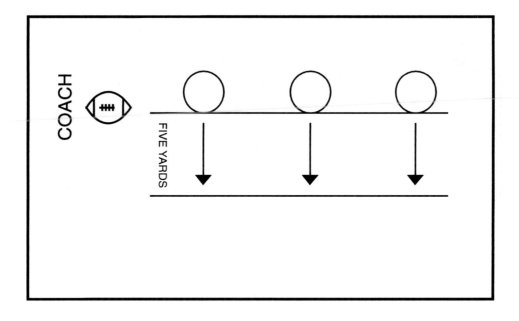

DRILL #5: WAVE

Objective: To warm-up; to enhance the player's reaction time.

Equipment Needed: A football.

Description: A player assumes a ready position and faces the coach. The player should be rapidly moving his feet in place. Holding the ball in front of his chest, the coach thrusts the ball in one of four basic directions (left, right, forward, and over his head). The player responds to the ball's movement by shuffling to the specified direction. A shuffle movement requires that the player step to the direction in which he is moving with his lead foot. A player never crosses his feet over when shuffling. To change directions when shuffling, a player should plant off the lead foot and change directions without wasted movement.

Coaching Points:

- When the coach moves the ball over his head, the player should sprint forward.

- The coach may establish a fifth dimension to the drill by establishing a neutral signal in which the player resumes the starting position—feet moving in place in the ready position. A commonly used neutral signal is having the coach hold the football at his chest.

- This drill should be done at varying speeds, depending on the time of practice.

- The coach should emphasize the importance of having each player focus on him in order to see his signal (the movement of the football).

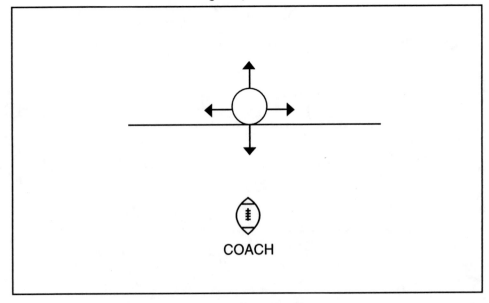

COACH

DRILL #6: SEAT ROLL

Objective: To warm-up; to enhance the player's reaction time.

Equipment Needed: None.

Description: A player assumes a ready position and faces the coach. The player should be rapidly moving his feet in place. On command from the coach, the player drops to the ground. The player should collapse a knee to drop to his hip. For example, to execute a seat roll to his right, the player should collapse his right knee and initially contact the ground with his right hip and buttock. In collapsing his right knee inward, the player should rotate the toe of his right foot to the inside. The coach visually signals to the player whether he should roll left or right. After a set number of repetitions, the coach gives the command "go," and the player sprints past him.

Coaching Points:

- This drill is appropriate for all defensive players.

- The player should keep his head up and his eyes focused on the coach.

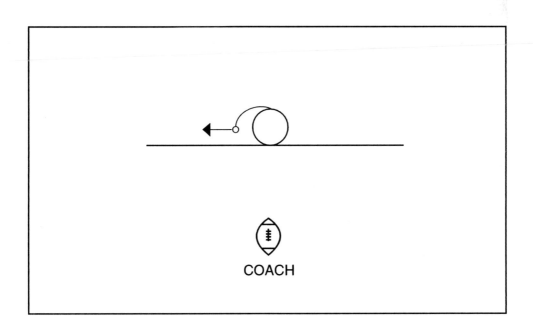

COACH

DRILL #7: QUARTER EAGLE

Objective: To warm-up; to enhance the player's reaction time.

Equipment Needed: None.

Description: A player assumes a ready position and faces the coach. The player should be rapidly moving his feet in place. On command from the coach, the player turns his feet and hips, first one way and then the other. The upper body should remain facing forward as the player's hips and feet quickly pivot and return to the forward facing position. After a sufficient number of repetitions, the coach gives the command to roll out. The players execute a forward roll and sprint past the coach.

Coaching Points:

- The drill is particularly appropriate for linebackers and defensive backs.

- Younger players should not execute a forward roll until they have demonstrated the ability to perform the forward roll technique properly.

- The player should continue moving his feet in short, choppy steps.

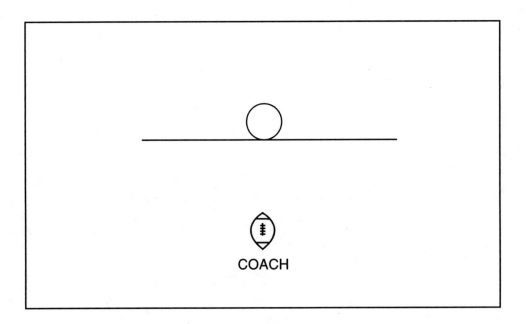

COACH

DRILL #8: TWIST-A-FLEX

Objective: To warm up, to enhance the defender's hip flexibility.

Equipment Needed: None

Description: The defensive back stands on a line and faces the coach. On the coach's command, the defensive back backpedals three steps and then begins to swivel his hips right and left. His legs and feet stay in line with the hips, acting as levers extending down from the hips. The defensive back continues backward as he uses the hip swivel movement to propel himself backward. The player should continue five to ten yards down the line.

Coaching Points:

- The player's feet and legs should stay in line with the hips. When the hips swivel right, the knees and the toes should swivel to the right as an extension of the hips.

- The backward movement of the player in this drill resembles a hopping movement incorporated with the hip swivel movement.

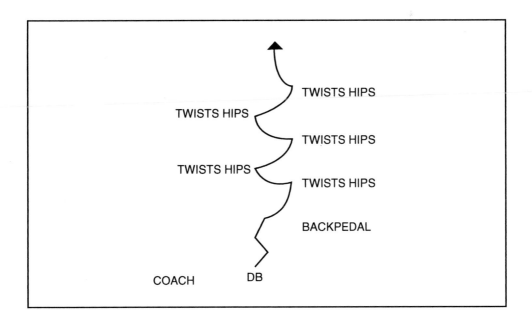

DRILL #9: SCISSORS KICK

Objective: To warm up; to develop the defender's hip flexibility.

Equipment Needed: None

Description: The defensive back stands on a line and faces the coach. On the coach's command, the defensive back runs down the line with a high bounding movement. The player should bring his lifted knee across the midline of his body as he bounds. He should put most of his weight on his toes as he bounds. He should reach out with his lead foot while still getting height from his bound. The player should continue five to ten yards down the line.

Coaching Points:

- This drill should be performed daily as part of the team's warm-up regimen.

- The knee should drive upward as the player moves forward.

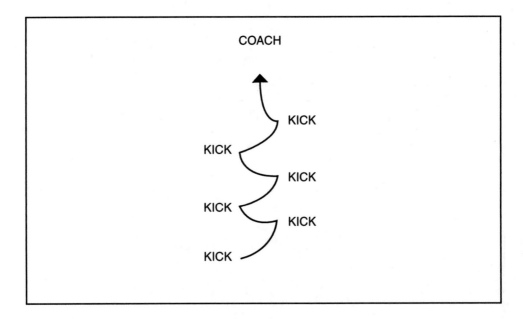

DRILL #10: SWIVEL HIPS

Objective: To warm-up; to enhance hip flexibility.

Equipment Needed: None

Description: The player assumes the ready position as he looks down a chalk line. On the coach's command, the player runs down the line. The player crosses over each time he steps, so that his steps alternate on either side of the line.

Coaching Points:

- The player should learn to keep his center of gravity over the line as he alternates his crossover steps.

- The player should run on the balls of his feet as he runs down the line.

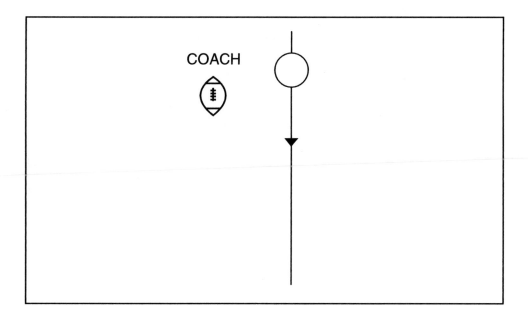

DRILL #11: READY TO PLAY

Objective: To reinforce the defender's ability to assume a proper stance.

Equipment Needed: None.

Description: The defenders line up in pairs, and one player assumes a blocking stance. The second player aligns over the blocker. Depending on the defensive position of the defender (i.e., defensive line, linebacker, or a defensive back using a bump and run technique), the defender assumes an appropriate defensive stance. On command from the coach, the defensive player relaxes and the coach checks the stance and the alignment of the defensive player. The defender must adhere to the proper fundamentals for stance and alignment at all times. After a number of repetitions, the players switch roles.

Coaching Points:

- Proper alignment (i.e., head on, inside/outside shoulder) and stance should be stressed at all times.

- The defender should adjust his alignment to the given split (i.e., distance from the nearest inside blocker).

- This exercise is an excellent "daily must" drill for youth-level players.

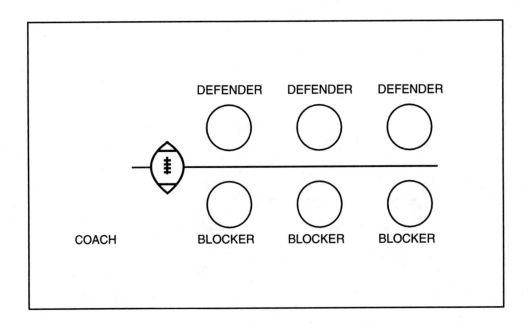

CHAPTER 2

AGILITY DRILLS

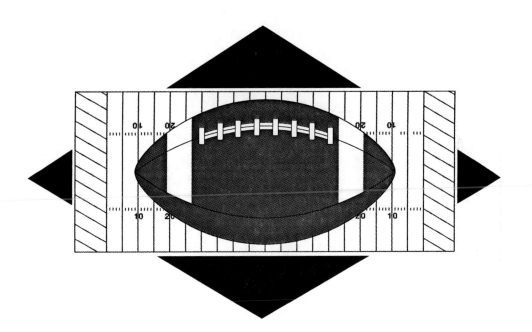

DRILL #12: LATERAL SLIDE

Objective: To warm-up; to enhance the ability of a defender to move laterally.

Equipment Needed: None.

Description: The player assumes the ready position and faces the coach. The coach directs the player to laterally slide one step in the direction he pointed. After sliding one step, the player comes to a complete stop and assumes the ready position. The coach again signals for the players to laterally slide one step in either direction. After a number of slides, the coach then points over his head to direct the player to sprint as fast as he can past him.

Coaching Points:

- The drill can be modified to require the player to continue to slide laterally until told to stop before he assume his defensive ready position.

- The coach should emphasize that the players maintain proper body positioning at all times during the drill.

- The coach should emphasize the importance of having each player focus on him in order to see his signal.

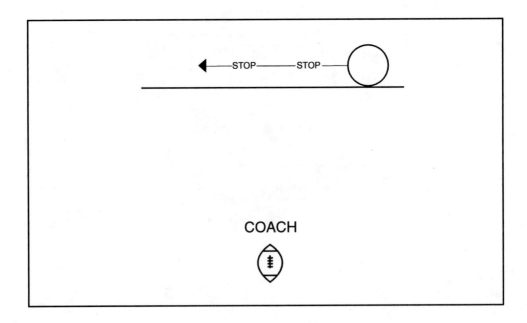

DRILL #13: CROSSOVER LATERAL RUN

Objective: To warm-up; to enhance the ability of a defender to run laterally.

Equipment Needed: None.

Description: The player assumes the ready position and faces the coach. The coach directs the player to run laterally in the direction he pointed. When the coach gives the command, the player comes to a complete stop and returns to the ready position. The coach again signals for the players to run laterally one in either direction. After a number of slides, the coach then points over his head to direct the player to sprint as fast as he can past him.

Coaching Points:

- The player should be positioned so that he can run down a chalk line. He should keep his shoulders square to the line as he runs laterally.

- Proper body positioning (i.e., hips, back, head, etc.) should be emphasized at all times during the drill.

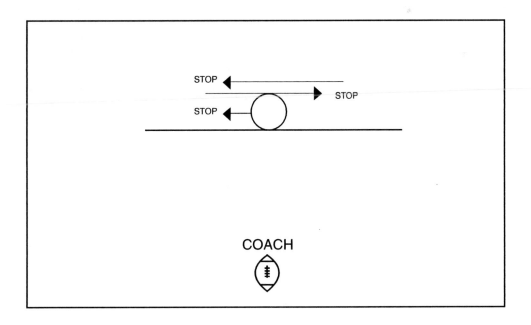

DRILL #14: HOT POTATO

Objective: To enhance the defender's ability to move laterally; to enhance the player's hand-eye coordination.

Equipment Needed: Two footballs.

Description: The coach starts this drill with a football in each hand. The player stands facing the coach from a distance of two to three yards away. The coach begins the drill by tossing one ball to the player. The player catches the ball and throws it back to the coach. As the ball is moving toward the coach, the coach immediately throws the second ball to the player. The second toss should force the player to move laterally to one side. The sequence continues as the sequence is repeated for a set amount of time (e.g., 20 seconds, etc.).

Coaching Points:

- The player should catch the ball using both hands. After catching the ball, the player should place a hand over the point of the ball, put it away, and then throw the ball back to the coach. He should not be allowed to bat the ball back to the coach.

- A player may be substituted for the coach to increase the player's repetitions. This is an excellent warm-up drill for players to practice on their own.

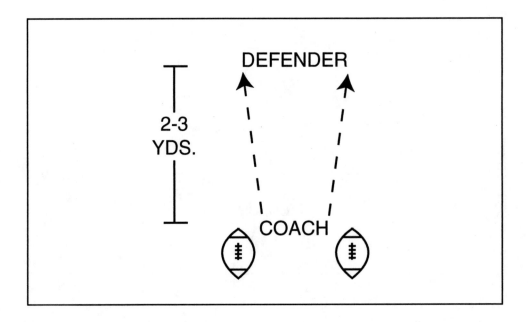

DRILL #15: ROPE JUMPING

Objective: To warm-up; to enhance a player's level of agility.

Equipment Needed: Jump ropes.

Description: The coach should start his team jumping rope daily, having his players jump using two feet at a time for the first month. The players should be allowed to rest as needed. During the second month, the players should be required to jump rope on leg for one minute, rest for twenty seconds, then repeat the sequence using the other leg. At the start of the third month, the players should be required to alternate legs for each jump (skipping).

Coaching Points:

- The coach should not expect players to progress rapidly with this drill. Rope jumping is a skill that takes time for some players to master.
- This drill is an excellent activity to use as a conditioning exercise, once the players have mastered the rudiments of jumping rope.

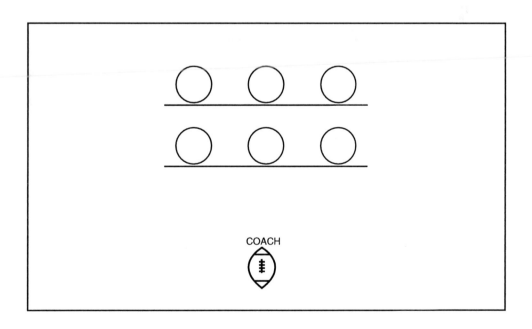

DRILL #16: SPINNING WHEEL

Objective: To warm-up; to enhance a player's level of agility from a three-point stance.

Equipment Needed: None

Description: A line of players spread out on a chalk line. The players assume a three-point stance and line up facing the coach. On the coach's movement, each player sprints five yards and places the palm of his right hand on the ground. He then turns a complete circle to his right and gets up to sprint five more yards. At the second five-yard increment, the player puts the palm of left hand down on the ground and turns a complete circle to his left. He then gets up to sprint the final five yards of the fifteen-yard distance.

Coaching Points:

- The coach should encourage the player to get his palm to the ground—less than four fingers on the ground is unacceptable.

- The players should keep their heads up while spinning on one hand.

- The coach may time an individual player to create a level of competition.

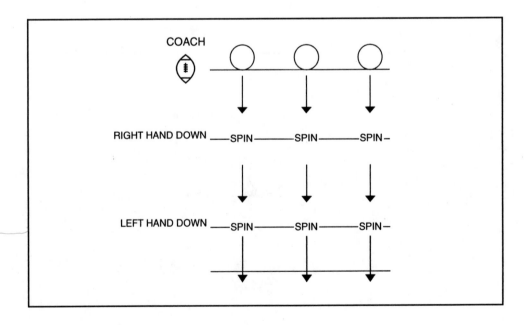

CHAPTER 3

FOOTWORK DRILLS

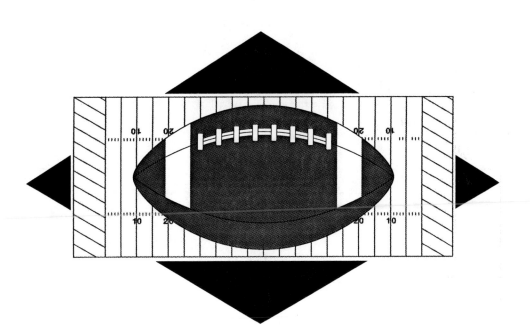

DRILL #17: BACKPEDAL AND FORWARD SPRINT

Objective: To warm up; to improve footwork.

Equipment Needed: None.

Description: The player assumes the ready position with his feet set close together. To effectively backpedal, a player must keep his feet set close together. The drill is set up so that the player backpedals five yards, then plants to sprint forward to the starting line. The player alternately backpedals and sprints forward for a specified number of repetitions. He should finish the drill by sprinting forward to simulate a tackle.

Coaching Points:

- This drill is an excellent exercise for linebackers and defensive backs. It also has some value for defensive linemen, bnecause it helps to develop hip flexibility.

- This drill is a good exercise to teach the defensive back how to "T" step. A "T" step is a technique that a defensive back uses to get a hard forward push when breaking from a backpedal.

- The player can be directed to overemphasize his forward lean by having him touch the ground with their front hand at the break point.

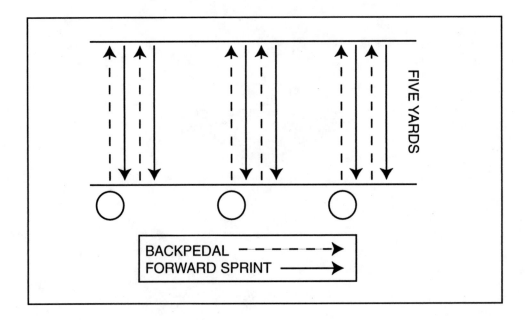

DRILL #18: STAGGERED BAG STEP

Objective: To warm-up; to improve footwork.

Equipment Needed: Four low-profile bags; a stand-up dummy.

Description: The four bags are placed on the ground so that the player can work "uphill" to simulate a tackle. The bags should be set close enough together for the player to easily move laterally through the bags without having to overstride. The player assumes a ready position and chops his feet. On the coach's command, the player moves laterally over the dummies. He should maintain a good hitting position (i.e., flat back, head up, hands low, etc.) as he works through the bags. A stand-up tackling dummy can be positioned several yards upfield from the last bag. Once the defender clears the last bag, he should move to execute a tackle on the stand-up dummy.

Coaching Points:

- If low-profile bags are unavailable, rolled-up towels may be used as the obstacle to step over.

- Several different lateral movement techniques can be used, including: a lead- step technique; a cross-over step technique; a two-steps-in-the-hole technique; and a two-steps-over-and-one-step-back technique.

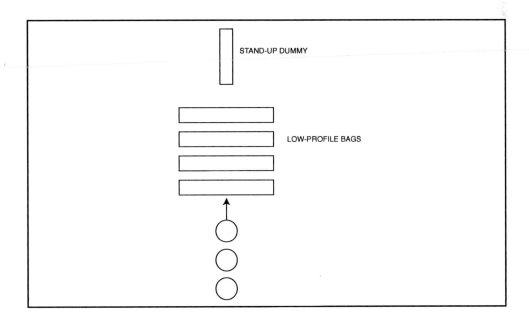

STAND-UP DUMMY

LOW-PROFILE BAGS

DRILL #19: RUNNING ROPES

Objective: To warm-up; to improve footwork.

Equipment Needed: Running ropes.

Description: A number of drills exist which involve the use of running ropes. Among the examples of some of the running rope drills are the following: require the player to run through with one foot in each square as he straddles the middle rope; run through with two feet in each square as he moves down one side of the middle rope; cross-over using every opening or every other opening; hop straddle every opening or every other opening, hop with both feet and hit every square; run diagonals with a left-foot lead step and then a right-foot lead step.

Coaching Points:

- The coach should vary the sequence of different methods of going through the running ropes.

- The running ropes can be removed from the frame and placed on the ground. This option is an excellent modification for emphasizing quick feet.

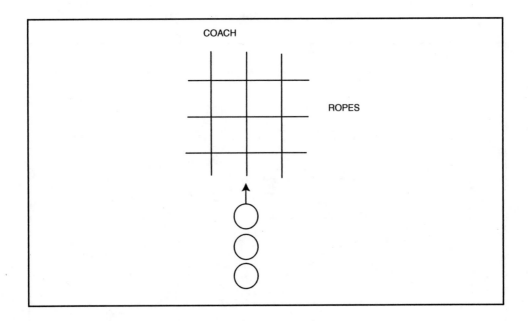

DRILL #20: BARREL SKIDS

Objective: To enhance footwork; to build stamina.

Equipment Needed: A plastic 55-gallon barrel; several cones

Description: A 55-gallon plastic drum is set on its side and several cones are positioned to layout a track. The player grasps the barrel by placing one hand on each end and locking out his arms. Holding the barrel out in this manner forces the athlete to arch his lower back and bend his knees. On the coach's command, the player churns his feet and pushes the barrel along the obstacle course. As long as the player sinks his hips and keeps the barrel out in front of him, the barrel will scoot along on its side. The player can turn the barrel and change his direction by using his leverage on the barrel and swing his tail around opposite the direction in which he wants to go. The player should keep his head up as he pushes the barrel along the ground.

Coaching Points:

- The ground should have a firm and smooth grass turf for the barrel to skid along the ground as it should.

- The coach should time the players to create a competitive environment.

- If the player doesn't keep his tail down and his arms locked out, the barrel will "buck" by sticking on the ground.

- The player must be required to scoot the barrel, and not allowed to roll it.

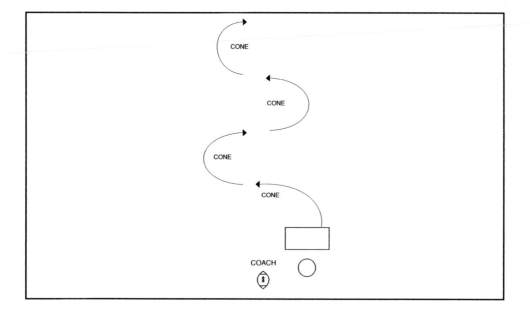

DRILL #21: POLE Z SEAT ROLLS

Objective: To improve footwork; to enhance stamina.

Equipment Needed: Two telephone poles approximately twelve feet in length.

Description: The two poles are positioned on the ground, parallel to each other. A line of players aligns at the end of one of the poles. On the coach's command, a player assumes a four-point stance on the outside of the pole. The player then shuffles over the pole in a lateral movement. His shoulders stay perpendicular to the pole as he crosses over. After he crosses over the first pole, he seat rolls with his head remaining forward. He comes out of the seat roll and crosses over the second pole. After he shuffles over the second pole in the same manner as the first, he seat rolls again on the outside of the pole. He then changes direction to cross the second pole and continue to seat roll in the middle. His movement continues back and forth in this manner making a "Z" pattern over the poles.

Coaching Points:

- The emphasis should be on quick moment of the feet and hands.

- The player should roll on his seat, not his back.

- The individual players can be timed to create a spirit of competition.

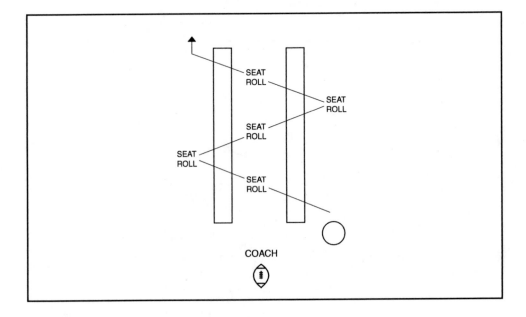

DRILL #22: POLE FLIPPER

Objective: To improve footwork; to enhance stamina.

Equipment Needed: Two telephone poles approximately twelve feet in length.

Description: The two poles are positioned on the ground, parallel to each other. A line of players aligns at the end of one of the poles. On the coach's command, a player assumes a four-point stance with his hands straddling the pole, but his feet together on the outside of the pole. On the coach's command, the player moves down the pole as fast as possible. As he continues down the pole, he keeps his hands straddling the pole while his feet weave back and forth from one side of the pole to another. At the end of the pole, the player seat rolls with his head facing his starting position; he then returns in the same fashion down the second pole.

Coaching Points:

- Variety can be added to the drill by having the player do essentially the same drill, except keep his feet straddled on the pole and flip his hands.

- The coach should enthusiastically encourage his players to keep the drill moving in a rapid fashion.

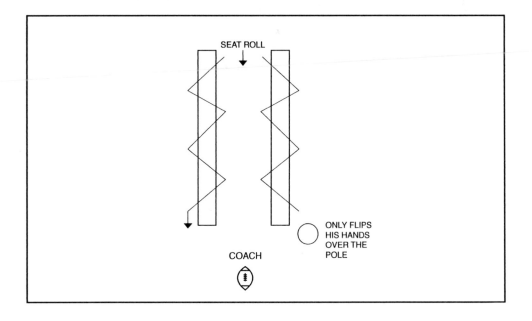

DRILL #23: THE BAG SHUFFLE

Objective: To improve footwork; to develop stamina.

Equipment Needed: Fifteen low-profile bags or rolled-up towels.

Description: Five bags are placed on the ground so that the player can work laterally over the bags. Three rows of five low-profile bags are set up so that three players can move through the bags at one time. A single row of bags should be set close enough together for the player to easily move laterally through the bags without having to overstride. The three players assume a ready position and chop their feet. On the coach's command, each player moves laterally over the bags. He should maintain a good hitting position (i.e., flat back, head up, hands low, etc.) as he shuffles over the bags. The coach should give the players a hand signal directing them to plant and shuffle the opposite direction. The players should get several commands to redirect their movement before given a signal to exit to the left or right. A lagging player may require the entire group to briefly repeat the drill.

Coaching Points:

- If low-profile bags are unavailable, rolled-up towels may be used as the obstacle to step over.

- Several different lateral movement techniques can be used, including: a lead- step technique; a cross-over step technique; a two-steps-in-the-hole technique; and a two-steps-over-and-one-step-back technique.

- The player should focus on the coach in order to see his signal.

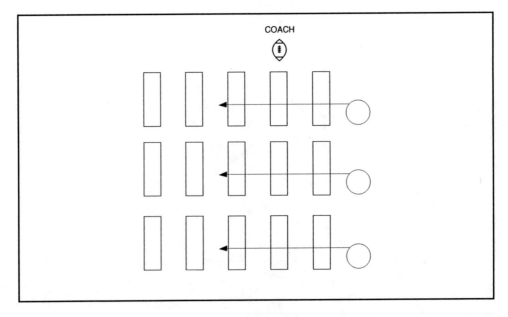

DRILL #24: YO - YO CHURNS

Objective: To warm up; to enhance the defensive back's footwork.

Equipment Needed: None

Description: The defensive back stands on a line and faces the coach. On the coach's command, the defensive back backpedals five yards. When he reaches the five-yard mark, the defender churns his feet to drive back to the starting point. The player should not stop when he reaches the five-yard mark. He should chop his feet and churn them to redirect his movement. He should keep his shoulders low and use his upper body to drive out of the backpedal.

Coaching Points:

- This is a daily must warm up drill for defensive backs.

- The player should use his arms and keep his elbows in as he backpedals and moves into the transition phase.

- The coach should avoid using the words "plant" and "stop" to refer to the direction change. The defensive back must churn his feet.

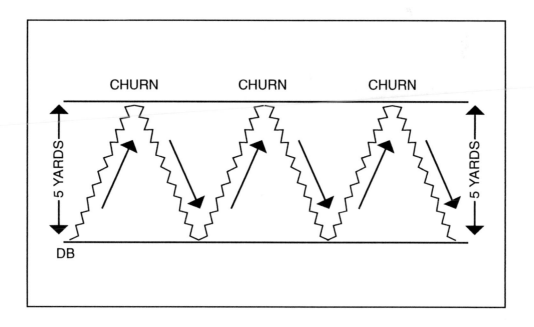

DRILL #25: QUICK–QUICK

Objective: To develop the defensive back's foot-churning technique when he's breaking out of his backpedal.

Equipment Needed: None

Description: A player stands on a yard-line and takes a good backpedal stance facing the coach. On the coach's movement, the player backpedals five yards. When the player reaches the five-yard mark, the coach gives the signal for "quick-quick". The quick-quick signal tells the player to churn his feet rapidly in place. When churning his feet in a quick-quick, the player keeps his feet close together. The coach allows the player to churn his feet for a only a second, then gives the player the signal to break forward. When the player returns to his starting point, the coach gives the player the second "quick-quick" signal. Again, the player churns his feet. The coach breaks him out of the quick-quick by giving him a signal to lateral shuffle down the line. The player is directed to shuffle two to three yards, then given a signal to shuffle back to the starting position. Upon returning to the starting position a second time, the player is directed to quick-quick. He is then given a signal to break forward past the coach after a moment of performing the quick-quick.

Coaching Points:

- This drill is an excellent exercise for teaching the defensive back to exhibit constant foot movement when making the transition from the backpedal to the drive to the ball.

- The coach should emphasize to the player to keep his shoulders low as he moves through the drill.

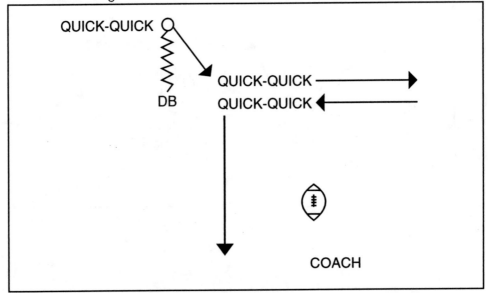

CHAPTER 4

CONDITIONING DRILLS

DRILL #26: YO-YO'S

Objective: To enhance the player's level of stamina.

Equipment Needed: None

Description: The coach has the entire defensive team spread out in three lines on the field facing him. One group is on the goal line, while the other two groups are on the ten-yard and twenty-yard line respectively. On the coach's command, the players run forward ten yards and touch the line, turn and sprint five yards back to the starting position, then turn and run forward ten yards. The players move forward a net distance of five yards on each repetition. The drill continues until the entire team has run the length of the field. The defensive backs should start at the goal line, the linebackers should start on the ten-yard line, and the defensive linemen should start on the twenty-yard line.

Coaching Points:

- If a particular player or group needs a greater handicap, the coach can increase the distance between groups.

- This drill can also be employed as an individual exercise to judge the movement ability and agility level of a player. The time it takes a player to negotiate a particular predesigned course (i.e., running from the goal line to the five-yard line and back, then from the goal line to the ten-yard line and back, etc.) could be measured.

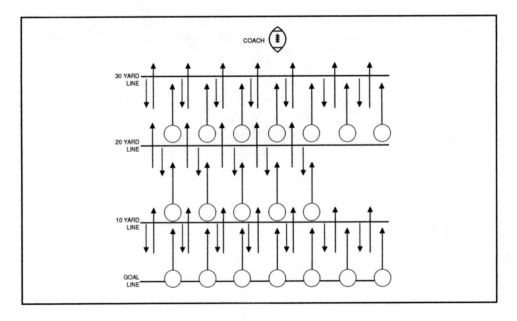

DRILL #27: FOUR CORNERS

Objective: To enhance the player's level of stamina.

Equipment Needed: Four cones.

Description: Four cones are positioned to form the four corners of a five-yard by five-yard box. The player backpedals down one side of the box to the first cone where he plants and shuffles laterally to the next cone. After reaching the second cone, the player sprints to the third cone. After reaching the third cone, the player shuffles laterally to the fourth cone—his original starting point.

Coaching Points:

- The drill can be repeated in a reverse direction so that the player finishes the drill with a straight ahead sprint.

- The coach can keep the group moving quickly by having the next player in line start as the previous player reaches the first cone.

- For maximum benefit, the coach should keep the groups to a small number of players.

- A player's performance can be timed in order to add a degree of competition to the drill and enhance the likelihood of improving a player's level of effectiveness.

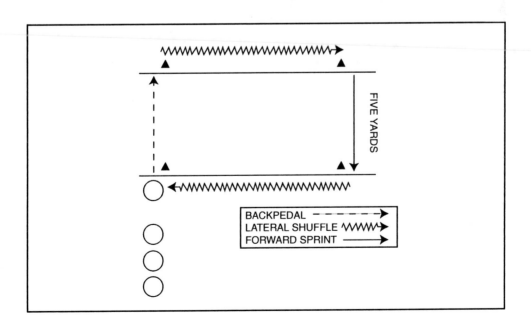

DRILL #28: RUSH AND COVER

Objective: To enhance the defensive lineman's level of stamina; to improve the ability of a defensive lineman to properly react to covering a thrown ball.

Equipment Needed: Four or five cones; a football.

Description: Depending on the number of participants, four to five cones are placed seven yards behind the line of scrimmage. A quarterback, a coach, or someone serving as a quarterback takes a deep snap from five yards back. The linemen rush to the cones as the ball is snapped. The quarterback throws a pass to a manager stationed ten to eleven yards downfield as the linemen reach their cones. When the linemen reach their cones, they immediately plant and sprint to the manager who caught the ball. If the linemen give full effort, the coach should blow the whistle early. Normally, a lineman who hustles should be required to run three to five yards past the line of scrimmage. This drill not only physically conditions the linemen, it mentally conditions them to turn and run to the direction in which a pass is thrown— thus getting eleven people to the ball, no matter what the nature of the play is.

Coaching Points:

- To simulate the two-minute drill conditions, the coach can require the drill continue for three to five plays in rapid succession before switching out the personnel.

- The coach should enthusiastically praise and reinforce the player's efforts.

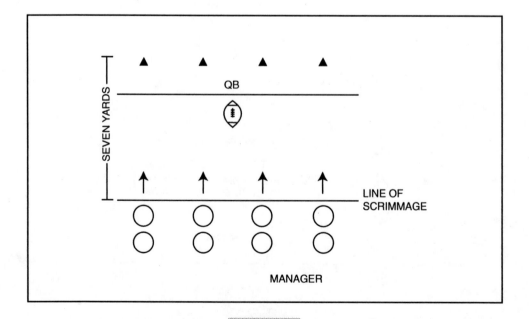

DRILL #29: TIRE DRILL

Objective: To develop the player's level of stamina; to increase his overall level of conditioning.

Equipment Needed: Twelve tires.

Description: Depending on the number of participants, nine to twelve tires are positioned three in a row with approximately three feet of distance between each tire. The rows of tires are approximately four yards apart, in order to give the players plenty of room. A series of tasks can be required of the player, tasks such as down and back; down and around; weave with tire on the left; weave with tire on the right; circle-circle; and half-turn at the top. The drill should be performed so that the next player in line goes as soon as the previous player returns to the starting point. This exercise is an excellent team or unit drill which builds camaraderie, as well as conditioning.

Coaching Points:

- Each position coach should be assigned a line to sponsor during the competition. This action can enhance the level of competitive spirit during the drill.

- This exercise is an excellent conditioning drill on which to finish practice.

- Tires are better than cones for two reasons. First, the diameter of the tire makes the player work harder on getting around the obstacle; second, tires cannot be knocked over as a tactic to slow down the drill.

- The tires should be inspected to make sure that steel threads are not protruding through the rubber.

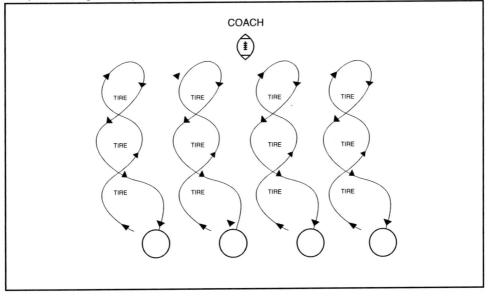

DRILL #30: PUNCH AND SLIDE

Objective: To build stamina; to enhance a defender's ability to play off a blocker using his hands.

Equipment Needed: Five-man sled.

Description: The players form a single line at the left end of the sled. One at a time, the players slide across the face of the sled. The first player shuffles down the sled striking each pad with the heel of each hand. A shuffling player should keep his left foot forward as he shuffles to the right. Each player should strike each pad with his thumbs pointing up. He should keep his head back and hold his elbows close to his sides. He should maintain a solid base under his body. The player may step into the pad with his forward foot to increase the punch to the pad. After each player has completed one repetition to the right, he reverses the direction while keeping the same technique. When moving to the left, the defensive player should keep his right foot forward. The coach should keep the line moving in a brisk manner.

Coaching Points:

- The coach should structure the drill so that adequate spacing between the players is maintained.

- In place of a five-man or seven-man sled, the drill may be run with five players holding shields.

- The player should punch the pads with great intensity, lifting the sled if possible.

- The drill may be developed into a conditioning-related activity by adding variation to the player's techniques. The player may skip every other pad, work two pads down and one pad back, seat roll between blow deliveries, etc.

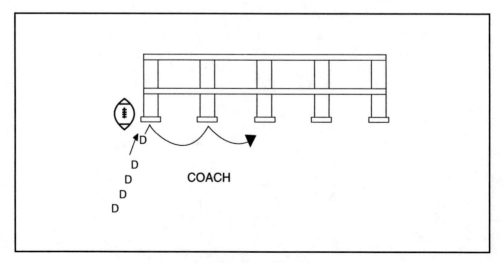

DRILL #31: PERFECT PURSUIT

Objective: To build stamina; to teach the defender to take the proper angle of pursuit.

Equipment Needed: A football; a five-man sled.

Description: A five-man sled is positioned in the middle of the field and the defensive unit aligns in front of the sled. A receiver is stationed on each sideline and a coach who acts as the quarterback positions himself behind the sled. A ball is used to cue the movement of the defensive line. On the simultaneous movement of the ball and the coach's command (cadence), the defensive line attacks the sled with the proper leverage while the second and third level defenders react to pass. The coach then throws a bullet pass to one of the receivers near the sideline. The players then take a pursuit angle to cut off the receiver as he jogs down the sideline. Each player should take an angle that allows him to tag the receiver on the shoulder. Each defensive position coach is directed to "judge" the stance, technique, pursuit angle, and effort of his people. If any player fails to rate acceptable in any of the categories, the repetition doesn't count. The head coach or defensive coordinator sets the number of perfect plays each day. A standard number of desired perfect plays is two to three.

Coaching Points:

- This drill is an excellent "bonding" exercise. Players soon realize they have to not only be responsible for themselves, but their teammates too.

- The coaches should not give advice or warnings to the players. Once the objective of the drill and the expectations are explained, the players should learn from their mistakes.

- The players' initial movement should be either on the movement of the ball or on the command (cadence) of the coach.

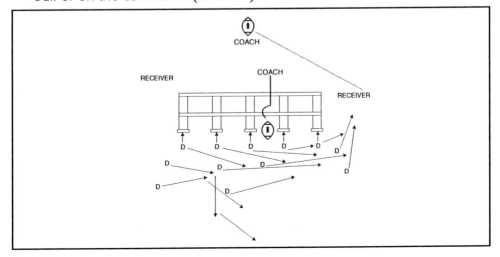

DRILL #32: RAPID PUNT COVER

Objective: To build stamina; to teach the defender to take the proper coverage lane.

Equipment Needed: A football; sixteen cones.

Description: Eight cones are aligned across the field. A second line of eight cones is aligned in a row approximately forty yards from the first line of cones. The defensive unit plays the role of the punt coverage team going against the "air". The ball is snapped a yard line in front of one set of cones and the front line of the punt coverage team steps to block a "ghost" defender. The head-hunters release from the line of scrimmage on the snap while the personnel responsible for protection count "one thousand and one, one thousand and two" and then release. The punt coverage teams sprints to where the cones are set up approximately thirty five yards downfield. When the individual player arrives at the individual cone, the player should break down into the ready position and chop his feet. A coach stands behind the cones and directs the players to shuffle along a horizontal plane. When the coach claps his hands, the players break out past the coach and reform in a huddle. The drill continues in the opposite direction.

Coaching Points:

- The coach should not delay the drill by attempting to coach the players in their alignment and assignment. The drill is designed to get a maximum number of repetitions in a short period of time.

- This drill is a good conditioning exercise because it gives the players additional practice at covering a punt.

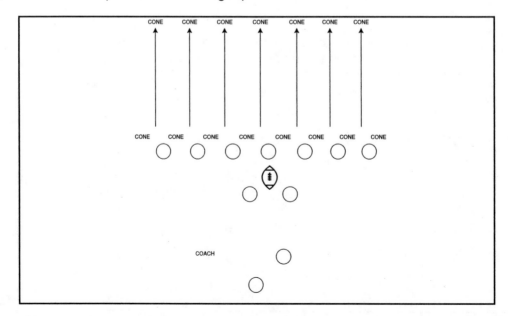

DRILL #33: SAVE THE TOUCHBACK

Objective: To build stamina; to teach the defender to ignore a punt receiver's fair catch signal inside the ten-yard line.

Equipment Needed: A football; thirteen cones.

Description: This drill can be run in a similar manner as drill #32-with cones designating the coverage lanes. The emphasis is on the head-hunter's technique. A head-hunter is a player who releases to cover the punt on the snap. A punt returner is stationed at the ten-yard line, and the ball is punted to a point near the goal line. The punt returner will give the fair catch signal and fake the fair catch. This is a common ploy to distract the head-hunters from their responsibility of downing the ball before it crosses the goal line. The head-hunters should ignore the fair catch signal and continue sprinting past the punt returner to down the ball.

Coaching Point:

- If the punt team is successful in downing the punt, the players can jog back to the original line of scrimmage. If the punt team is unsuccessful in downing the punt, the punt team should immediately set up for a tight punt from the one-yard line.

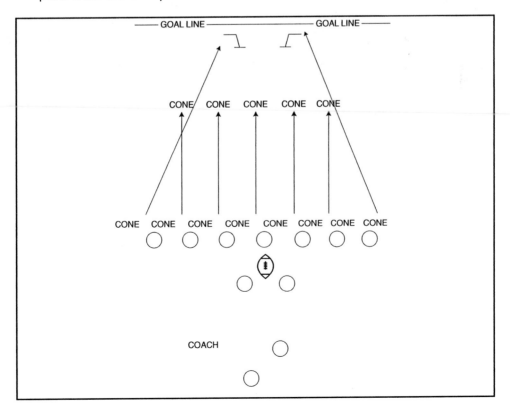

CHAPTER 5

BLOW
DELIVERY
DRILLS

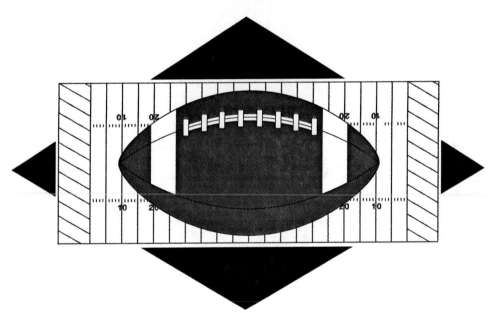

DRILL #34: HANDS ATTACK

Objective: To develop the defender's ability to deliver a blow with his hands and to fit to the blocker with his hat in his responsible gap.

Equipment Needed: A football; a five-man sled anchored by metal stakes.

Description: A player aligns in front of each pad on the anchor sled. All of the players align in the same technique, either an inside shade or outside shade. To cue movement, the coach either has the players either move on the ball or start on his command (cadence). On the movement of the ball, the players get off on the ball and use their hands to deliver a blow the pad. The players should hold their position on the sled after striking the pad and locking out their arms, so that the coach can evaluate their landmark. The player's neck should be bowed, and his eyes should be looking up. When the players use the hands technique, the player's head will not fit tightly to the pad, as his head will be back away from the pad because of his lock-out of the arms. Even when using his hands, the player's head will remain on a line intersecting the side of the pad, just farther back from the pad. He should be in a "football position" on the sled; knees bent, back straight, hips flexed, with his feet set shoulder-width apart underneath his body. The coach gives the command to release and the players reset and change their technique alignment.

Coaching Points:

- The sled is anchored, therefore the players should emphasize the upward strike of the sled, making the pad rise into the air.

- The players should work together so that they strike the sled in unison.

- When using the hands-blow delivery method, the defensive lineman should strike the pad with the heels of his hands. His fingers should be curled inward slightly. His elbows should be within the plane of his shoulders.

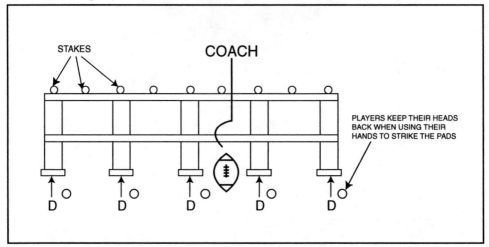

DRILL #35: PAD ATTACK

Objective: To develop the defender's ability to deliver a blow with his shoulder and to fit to the blocker with his hat in his responsible gap.

Equipment Needed: A football; a five-man sled anchored by metal stakes.

Description: A player aligns in front of each pad on the anchor sled. All of the players align in the same technique, either an inside shade or outside shade. To cue movement, the coach has the players either react to the movement of the ball or to his command (cadence). On the movement of the ball, the players get off on the ball and use the shoulder blow delivery technique to attack the pad. The players should hold their position on the sled after completing the forearm and shoulder-blow delivery so that the coach can evaluate their landmark. The players landmark should be a tightly fitted headgear to the pad of the sled. His earhole should be in contact with the side of the pad, his neck should be bowed, and his eyes should be looking up. He should be in a "football position" on the sled; knees bent, back straight, hips flexed, with his feet set shoulder-width apart underneath his body. The coach gives the command to release and the players reset and change their technique alignment.

Coaching Points:

- The sled is anchored, therefore the players should emphasize the upward strike of the sled, making the pad rise into the air.

- The players should work together so that they strike the sled in unison.

- The defensive lineman should strike the pad with his wrist positioned so that his palm faces his chest and his thumb points up.

- The coach should alternate standing in front of the sled and behind the sled to check the various points of each player's technique.

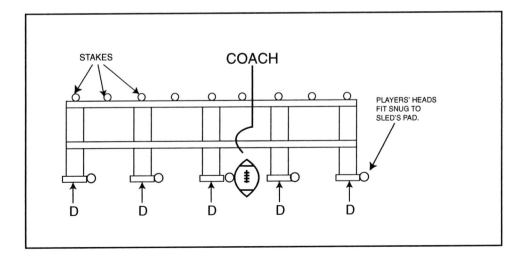

DRILL #36: TWO-MAN SLED ATTACK

Objective: To develop the defensive lineman's ability to throw the hands in an upward thrust.

Equipment: A football; a two-man sled (this drill is perhaps best performed when using an older model, stiff Crowther-style sled).

Description: Two defensive lineman kneel approximately 18 inches away from the pad of the sled. The defensive linemen should sit back on their heels, keep their upper body erect and bow their neck so that their head is back. The ball is moved by another coach or a player (if the number of available coaches is limited) so the coach is able to see the drill and observe the hand placement, elbow angle, and hip snap of the defenders. On movement of the ball, the defenders violently throw their hands into the pads. Initially, the blow is made without hip or leg extension for several repetitions. The drill progresses as the defenders are required to strike a blow and follow with the hips, knocking the sled backward so that the player is able to "lay out" in front of the dummy upon finishing the blow delivery. The players immediately recover and present themselves ready for another repetition.

Coaching Points:

• When laying out on the blow delivery, the player's body should contact the ground in this sequence; lower thigh, upper thigh, belt line, navel, and finally, the upper abdomen. Observing this sequence of contact on the ground gives the coach a foolproof read that the athlete is properly developing the technique.

• The sled should fly upward and outward. No player or coach should stand on the sled; the sled should be kept as light as possible to increase the psychological benefit of the sled being knocked up into the air.

• The players should attack the sled with the heel of their hands, thumbs up, use a chuck grasp, and keep the elbows in.

• The drill can also be started on the command (cadence) of the coach.

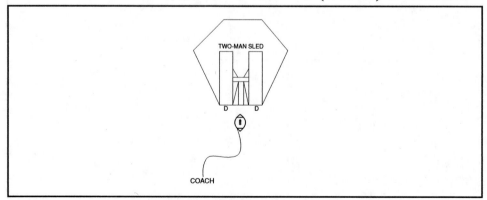

DRILL #37: THROW THE HANDS

Objective: To develop the defensive player's technique of using his hands to separate from a blocker.

Equipment: A football; two hand shields, two free-standing tackling dummies.

Description: The players form two lines. A teammate who is holding a hand shield just above his knee stands in front of the defensive player. The coach kneels between the players and moves the ball. On the movement of the ball, each defender gets off on the movement and throws his hands into the hand shield. The defender should strike the shield with the heel of his hand and drive the shield upward. The defender should drive the shield holder backward for two yards, then release and sprint to a free-standing tackling dummy located at a point three yards to his outside. The defensive lineman should execute a form tackle on the dummy.

Coaching Points:

- The coach should emphasize the explosive punch of the hands and check to make sure that the hand shield is being driven upward from the punch.

- The drill may be done live by players wearing shoulder pads.

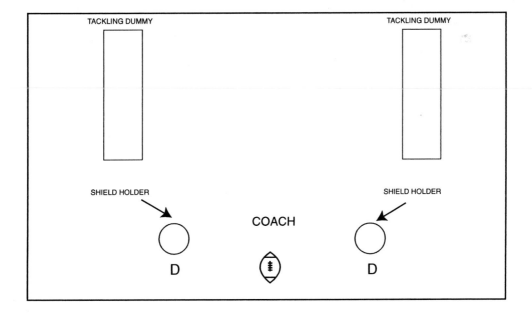

DRILL #38: SHOULDER BLOW DELIVERY

Objective: To isolate and practice the upper body technique of a shoulder blow.

Equipment Needed: A football; a hand shield.

Description: A player aligns in front of the shield holder. The shield holder bends his knees so that the shield is held low near his knees. The coach kneels nearby and moves the football to cue the defender's reaction. On the ball's movement, the defender drives his shoulder to the face of the shield. The shoulder blow should lifts the shield and knock the shield holder backward. A down defender operating from a three-or a four-point stance should land on his belt buckle and execute a seat roll to the side of the his free shoulder.

Coaching Points:

- Proper hip extension will result in the defensive lineman's upper body hitting the ground in progression from belt buckle to shoulders.

- The shield should be hit at an upward angle, and the shield holder should be knocked backward.

- This drill is a good exercise to train the front line and second-level players to play aggressively.

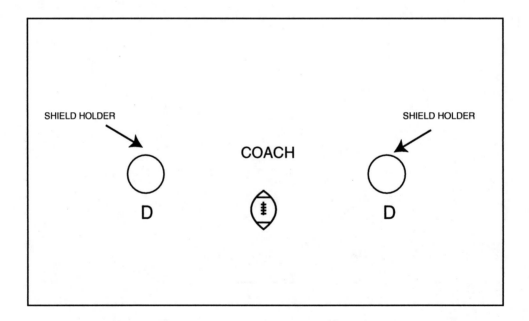

DRILL #39: SHUFFLE AND JAM

Objective: To develop the defender's ability to use his hands to jam a cut blocker and drive him into the ground.

Equipment Needed: A hand shield.

Description: A line of four to five blockers align in a stagger approximately five yards in front of the defender who is holding a shield. The shield holder bends his knees so that the shield is held low near his knees. On the coach's command, the first player takes off on angle to cut the defender's outside knee. The defender slides to the outside and positions himself so that he defender can shoot his shield to the blocker's head and shoulders. The defender uses the shield to protect himself and push the blocker's head and shoulders downward. The defender should attempt to work himself upfield as he defeats each blocker.

Coaching Points:

- The defender should keep his knees bent and his back as erect as possible.

- The blocker should wait until the defender defeats the previous blocker before attacking the defender.

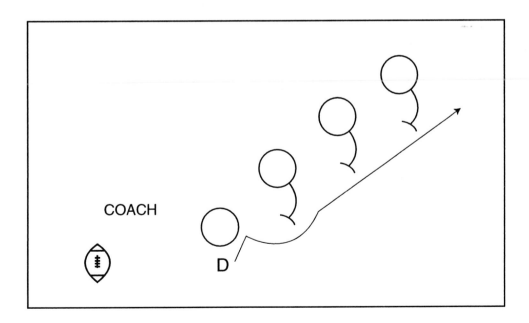

DRILL #40: SHOOT AND SLIDE

Objective: To develop the defender's ability to use his hands to jam a cut blocker and drive him into the ground.

Equipment Needed: None.

Description: A line of five to six blockers kneel down on all fours align with their hands on a chalk line. The players align approximately two feet from each other while a defensive player assumes the ready position at one end of the line. On the coach's command, the end blocker lunges forward toward the defender's knees and feet. The defender shoots both hands to the shoulders of the blocker and push him to the ground. As the defender jams the blocker's shoulders, he slides laterally down the line of blockers. Each blocker lunges for his feet and knees as the defender slides with his hands held low.

Coaching Points:

- The defender should keep his knees bent.

- The defender should keep his backside leg forward as he slides down the line.

- The defender should step into the blocker as he jams the blocker's shoulders backward.

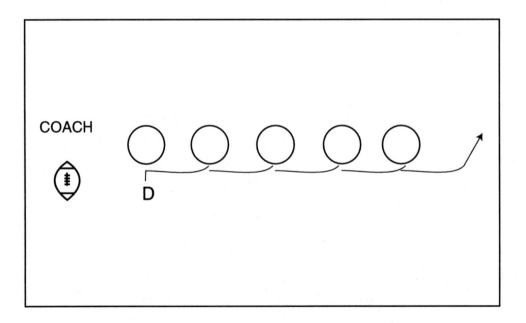

DRILL #41: BREAK THE STALK

Objective: To develop the defensive back's ability to use his hands to bench press the receiver away from his body and push him back to the inside to squeeze the alley.

Equipment Needed: None.

Description: Two players are positioned on the perimeter. One player acts as a wide receiver/blocker and the other as a defensive back. The defender assumes the proper stance and alignment for his cushion zone coverage technique. On the coach's command, the wide receiver gets off on the snap and attempts to stalk block the defender. To improve the defender's run playing technique, the coach simulates a run read by moving down the line of scrimmage. The defender plants off his backpedal and forms the second containment alley by attacking the receiver while keeping outside leverage.

Coaching Points:

- The defender should try to get his hands on the blocker's numbers, keep his head above the blocker's, and push the blocker back while maintaining outside leverage.

- The defensive back should attempt to work up through the blocker's pads and face to control him.

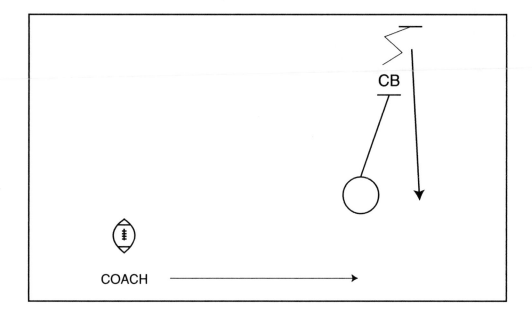

DRILL #42: FORCE THE ALLEY

Objective: To develop the force defender's ability to squeeze the running alley between the defensive end and the primary force.

Equipment Needed: None.

Description: The drill involves planning for groups of four. Two players act as pulling guards, while the other two are designated as defensive backs. The drill begins by having the four players set up facing each other across the line of scrimmage in their normal offensive and defensive stance and alignment. On the coach's command, one guard pulls and attempts to kick out the force. A force is a defender who forms the perimeter boundary for the pursuit of the defensive front. The closer the force is able to set the outer limit of the alley, the tighter the alley and the easier it is for the defensive front pursuit to fill the alley. After the force defender on one side of the ball has had a repetition, the second force defender and guard on the other side of the ball get a repetition. The defensive back or outside linebacker is normally the force. He should use his shoulder pad and hands to attack the guard and keep outside leverage.

Coaching Points:

- The defender should meet the guard as close to the center of the line of scrimmage as possible. If the ball carrier attempts to get around the force, he should force the ball carrier deeper.

- The defender should never meet a kick out blocker deeper than two yards behind the line of scrimmage.

- The defender should use his quickness and faking ability to make it difficult for the guard to get a solid block on him.

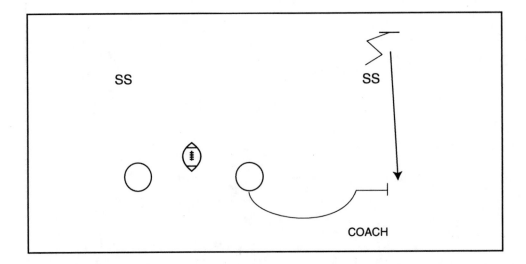

DRILL #43: SLED STINGERS

Objective: To reinforce the physical nature of attacking an opposing player.

Equipment Needed: An anchored five-man sled.

Description: The players are positioned at one end of the sled. The first player assumes a position approximately three yards from the first pad. On the coach's command, the first player attacks the sled with his right shoulder pad. After he hits the pad and drives it upward, he immediately backpedals to the three yard depth in front of the second pad and attacks. As the first player is backpedaling to the three-yard position in front of the second pad, the second player aligns at the three-yard starting point in front of the first pad. The two players then attack the sled in unison. The drill continues with the players attacking the sled and moving down the line. The sled is lifted up by the simultaneous contact. The sled drops back to the ground as the player's disengage the pad and backpedal to the three-yard point. The coach may develop the drill to a noncommand drill. If given no command, the players learn to work down the sled rhythmically so that the players contact the sled in unison. The direction of the players is switched and the drill is repeated.

Coaching Points:

- Players should quickly move off the sled at the highest point of the sled's lift.

- The coach should stand behind the sled to ensure that the players have their head up at the moment of contact.

- If anchoring the sled is not possible, the players should all align in front of each pad and attack the pad as a team instead of a rhythmic progression.

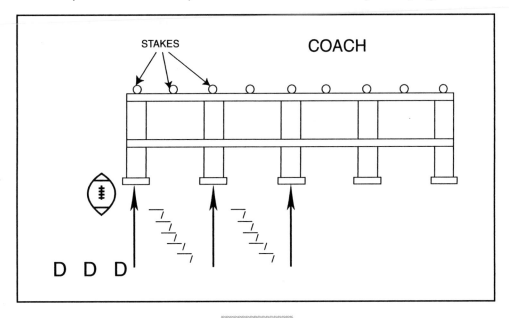

DRILL #44: BUCKER SHUFFLE

Objective: To improve the defender's ability to protect his legs and knees from a cut block.

Equipment Needed: A bucker station.

Description: A bucker is a teaching tool consisting of a padded board approximately six inches wide that is attached to several posts. The posts should be positioned behind the board so that the padding faces the players. The board should be anchored so that it is approximately thirty inches above the ground. A line of players is positioned at one end of the bucker. Each player slides laterally down the board, delivering hand shivers to the board as he moves. At the end of the board, the player should seat roll and return quickly to his feet.

Coaching Points:

- The player should strike the bucker squarely with the heels of his hand.

- The player should keep his thumbs up as he contacts the pad.

- The player should keep his elbows bent and his lower back arched as he shuffles down the bucker.

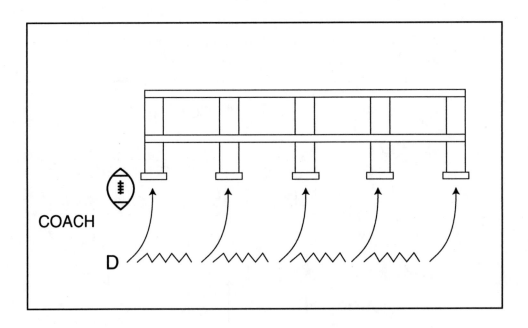

CHAPTER 6

REACTION DRILLS

DRILL #45: TAKE-OFF

Objective: To enhance the ability of a defensive lineman to react quickly and take an explosive first step to attack to the line of scrimmage.

Equipment: A football.

Description: The defensive linemen form two lines facing the football. Each player assumes a three-point stance. The coach kneels between two lines of players and moves the ball. On the movement of the ball, the defensive linemen take off and sprints two to three yards ahead. Each player should push off his front foot and take a big first step as he explodes from his stance.

Coaching Points:

- The coach should check the stance of each player.

- The coach should provide input to each player on the length of his first step.

- This drill is designed to be a "daily must" drill for defensive linemen.

- Requiring the defender to react to the movement of a football is designed to sharpen the defensive lineman's concentration on the ball's movement.

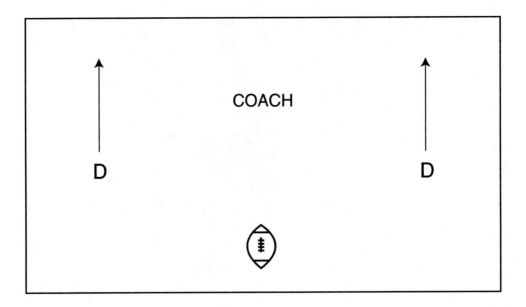

DRILL #46: REACT AND MIRROR

Objective: To develop the player's ability to react to the movement of an offensive player.

Equipment: A football; two cones.

Description: Two cones are placed on the ground approximately seven yards apart. A player simulating a ball carrier stands approximately five yards in front of the cones. A defensive player assumes the ready position between the ball carrier and the cones. The ball carrier moves from side to side as he attempts to get past the defender. The defensive player mirrors the ball carrier, staying between him and the cones. The defender's objective is to prevent the ball carrier from scoring (i.e., crossing the line). The defender should put his hands behind his back. The ball carrier should be given a specific time limit (e.g., 8 seconds) in which to score.

Coaching Points:

- To provide another feature to the drill, the defender may be allowed to use his hands.

- When using his hands, the defender should not overextend his arms.

- The drill should emphasize foot quickness, body control, and proper positioning.

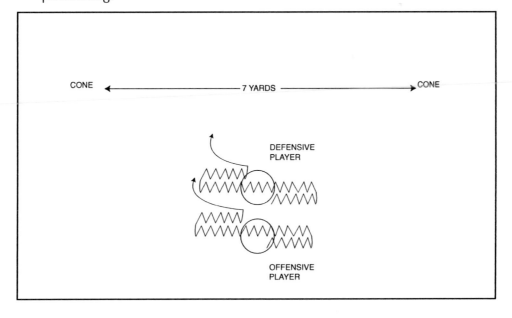

DRILL #47: REACT AND GO

Objective: To warm-up and practice an effective pass rushing angle.

Equipment Needed: A football; two cones or blocking dummies.

Description: The drill involves the coach and three players. Representing interior offensive linemen, two cones (or blocking dummies) are set up five yards apart on a yard line. Standing between the cones, the coach snaps the ball to an individual serving as a quarterback. On movement of the ball, the two defenders sprint low and hard across the line of scrimmage and take the proper angle to the quarterback who is positioned six yards behind the cones.

Coaching Points:

• In this drill, the pass rushers can practice stripping the quarterback. When adding this feature to the drill, the coach should instruct the quarterback simulator to hold the ball back in a throwing motion.

• The pass rushers should alternate so that they do not accidentally run into each other.

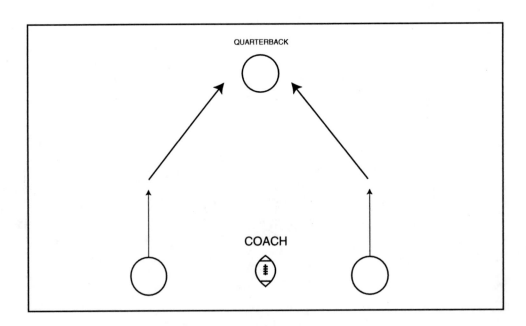

DRILL #48: THE DOOR

Objective: To warm-up; to help the player develop the fundamentals of tackling.

Equipment Needed: A free-standing door; two cones; several footballs.

Description: The door is positioned so that a line of players face each side. One line of players simulates the ball carrier while the other line of players assume the role of a defensive player. The front player of each line is positioned approximately ten feet from the door. On the coach's command, the defensive player assumes the ready position and chops his feet in place. The ball carrier moves three steps toward the door then breaks to one side of the door. The defender should remain in the ready position until the ball carrier runs into view. Once the ball carrier moves into view, the defender should move toward the ball carrier on a proper tackling angle. The defender should use his hands to deliver a shiver to the ball carrier and simulate a tackle.

Coaching Points:

- This drill should be run at a slow controlled pace—approximately half speed.

- The emphasis should be on the defender eliminating any false step while breaking to ball carrier.

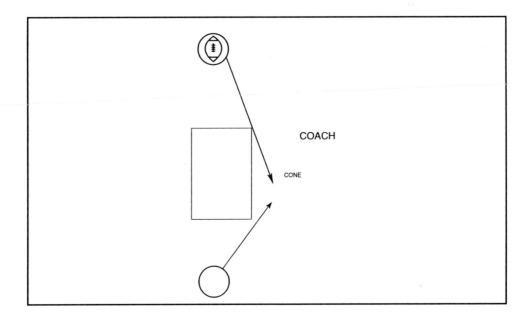

DRILL #49: REACT AND CATCH

Objective: To develop hand coordination and quickness.

Equipment Needed: One Nerf football; two tennis balls.

Description: The drill involves two players, a coach, and someone to simulate a snap. As the ball is snapped, the players' eyes focus on the tennis balls that are being held by the coach who is positioned three yards from the snapper. Holding his arms out from his body (forming a "T"), the coach drops the tennis balls. The players react to the dropping of the tennis ball on their particular side and try to catch the ball before it hits the ground a second time on the bounce. After each player has had success from a distance of three yards from the coach, the players can move back to four yards, etc. A depth of five to six yards from the coach is considered especially challenging. The coach should be particularly alert once the competitive level is increased and players start diving for the tennis balls.

Coaching Points:

- The key to the player experiencing success is his ability to react to the snap of the Nerf ball and to move quickly to catch the falling tennis ball.

- Once the player becomes proficient at reacting to and going for tennis balls, the coach can switch to using footballs.

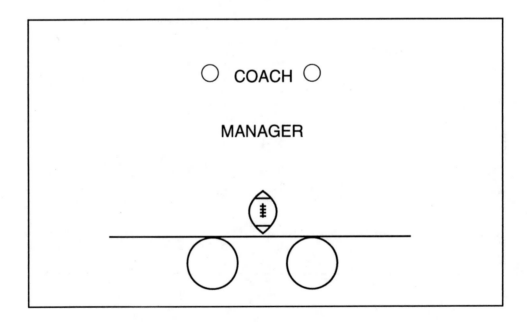

DRILL #50: BIG RED SHUFFLE

Objective: To develop the player's ability to use his hands to react to a cut blocker and protect his legs.

Equipment Needed: A football; a Big Red Ball

Description: The Big Red Ball is a coaching aide that is approximately 42" in diameter. One of the more common brands is the color red. The surface of the ball is textured with slight bumps so that the ball is more easily controlled by the coach and the player. The coach rolls the Big Red Ball at the lineman's outside leg. The player shuffles to the outside and keeps his outside foot back as he focuses on the ball. He then strikes the ball with the heel of his hands to knock it back to the coach. At this point, the player then returns to his starting position. The coach pushes the ball into the outside leg of the defender for several repetitions. Players who play on the right side should work with their right foot back. Players who play on the left side should work with their left foot back.

Coaching Points:

- The coach should encourage the player to shift his focus to the ball as he is striking the ball.

- Once the player strikes the ball, he should again focus on the coach.

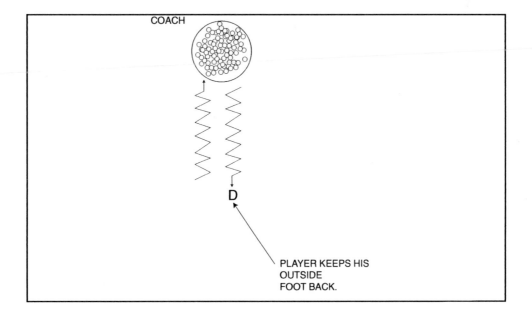

DRILL #51: REACT AND ACT

Objective: To teach defenders to react properly to a cutoff or angle block.

Equipment Needed: A defensive reactor sled.

Description: The drill involves having a defensive lineman or a linebacker assume his proper defensive stance one yard in front of a defensive reactor sled. A coach stands on the defensive reactor sled and operates a lever which triggers the sled pads. After the defensive player is positioned in his stance, the coach will trigger the pad release mechanism on the sled. The defender must react quickly, striking the pad with his backside shoulder and flipper and keeping his "playside" arm free. If the pad to the defender's right fires forward, the defender should keep his right shoulder free as he moves to strike the pad with his left shoulder and flipper. When striking the reactor pad, he should step with his backside leg to add leverage and force to his blow.

Coaching Points:

- A free-standing tackling dummy can be placed to either side of the reactor sled so that the defensive player can finish the drill with a form tackle.

- The defender should not false step as he slides to keep "playside" leverage on the reactor pad.

- The defender should keep his shoulders square when he strikes the sled.

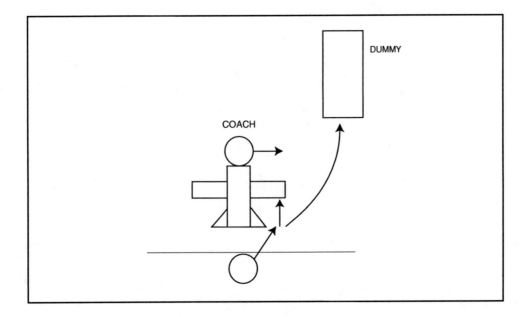

DRILL #52: REACT TO THE CRACK

Objective: To teach second and third level defenders to react to a crack back block.

Equipment Needed: A football; a free-standing dummy.

Description: The defender assumes his proper stance on the side of his normal alignment from the ball. A large free-standing dummy is positioned to the outside of the defender. The coach plays quarterback and comes down the line of scrimmage, simulating a speed option. He pitches the ball quickly to a trailing running back. The defender must take his regular read step and then react to the wide play. The player who is next in line for the drill should yell "crack-crack-crack" to the first defender. The defender should get peek outside to locate the dummy and rip his inside arm and shoulder "across the top". By playing over the top of the dummy, the defender learns to give ground against a crack back blocker and not be captured. This drill is a very effective teaching situation when the dummy is replaced by a live blocker holding a hand shield.

Coaching Points:

- This drill is most appropriate for linebackers and defensive backs.

- The defender should keep his shoulders square as he clears the crack back blocker.

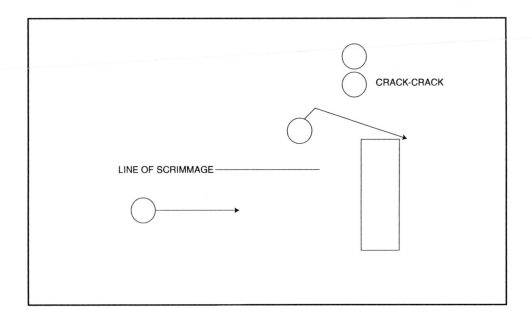

DRILL #53: HALF COVERAGE

Objective: To develop the defensive back's ability to play the ball in the air from a deep half-zone responsibility.

Equipment Needed: A football.

Description: Two receivers align on the hash marks. The coach stands midway between the hash marks and holds the football. The defensive back aligns directly in front of the coach, approximately twelve yards from the line of scrimmage. On the coach's signal, each receiver streaks down the hash. The defensive back backpedals straight back to keep his cushion until he is forced to turn the outside. If he is forced to turn outside, the deep half zone defender should keep his head over his inside shoulder to look at the football. Once the coach throws the ball, the defender should break on the pass and intercept the pass at its highest point.

Coaching Points:

- The coach should alternate throwing the ball deep to either receiver.

- The coach should vary the depth of the pass, occasionally throwing the ball before the defender has time to flip his hips.

- The coach should hang the ball in the air to give the defender confidence in his ability to effectively cover the half zone.

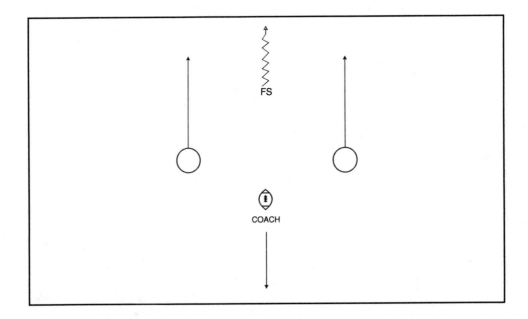

DRILL #54: THROW AND CATCH

Objective: To improve the defender's ability to concentrate on catching the football.

Equipment Needed: A football.

Description: Several players form a semi-circle. One player stands in the middle of the semi-circle and faces the group. The player in the middle and the first player in the semi-circle both have a football. The drill begins by having the middle man pass to the second player as the first player passes his ball to the middle man. This pattern is repeated around the semi-circle until both footballs have been passed to the last player. The process should then be continued back to the beginning stage of the drill.

Coaching Points:

- This drill is appropriate for linebackers and defensive backs.

- Competition can be added to the drill by having the player count the number of times that thrown balls are caught by each player.

- The coach should emphasize utilizing proper techniques at all times (i.e., a player catches the ball, places his fingertips over the point of the ball, put it into his body and employs cross body action). Cross body action involves the player using his arm and body to protect the ball across the front of his body.

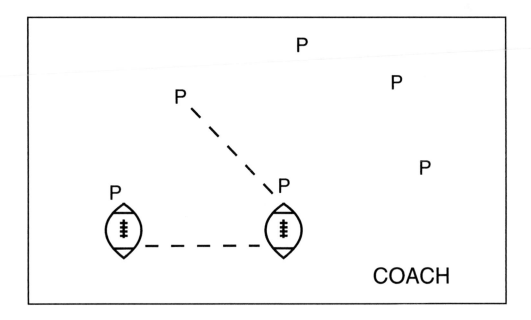

DRILL #55: KNEE DROPS

Objective: To develop the defender's level of agility; to enhance the ability of a defender to react to a visual cue.

Equipment Needed: None.

Description: A player aligns four to six yards in front of the coach and assumes the ready position. On the coach's command, the player should begin chopping his feet. The coach then uses either hand to point at the player's knee. If the coach points to the player's left knee, the defender quickly drops to his left knee and pops back up to the ready position. If the coach points to the player's right knee, the defender quickly drops to his right knee and again pops back up to the ready position. The drill continues for a set amount of time (e.g., 20 seconds, etc.).

Coaching Points:

- The player should keep his feet moving when he is in the ready position.
- The coach should make his hand signals quick but clear.
- The drill should be done either with players wearing knee pads or on a padded surface.

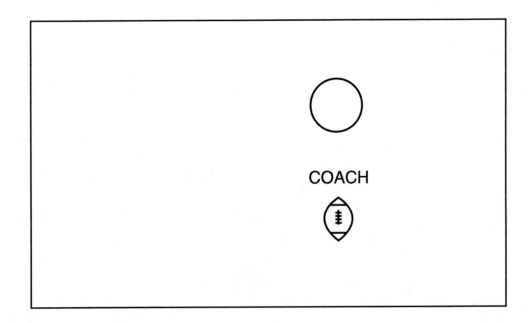

CHAPTER 7

READ DRILLS

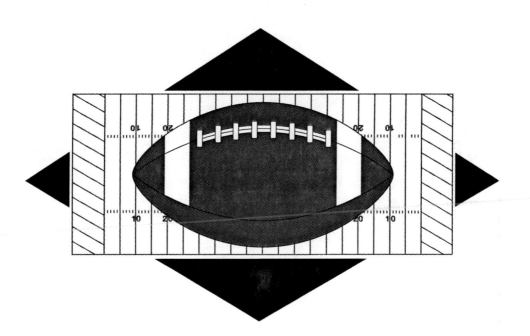

DRILL #56: BRIGHT LIGHTS ON

Objective: To enhance the ability of an inside linebacker to read the offensive lineman as his primary key and to react properly.

Equipment Needed: Two free-standing dummies.

Description: The linebacker assumes his proper stance on the side of his normal alignment from the ball. A large free-standing dummy is positioned to each side of the offensive lineman. The linebacker focuses on the top screws of the offensive lineman's facemask. He should also be able to interpret the angle of the first step of the offensive lineman.. On the movement of the offensive lineman, the linebacker takes a read step and instantly reads the intention of the blocker. If the blocker fires off on a cutoff angle, the linebacker works to keep his "playside" shoulder and arm free as he attacks the free-standing dummy to that side. If the blocker fires off straight ahead on the linebacker, he attacks the dummy which corresponds to his primary gap responsibility on a "flow to" read. If the offensive lineman angle blocks inside or outside, the linebacker fires straight ahead if the offensive lineman pops up to show pass, the linebacker dropsteps and freezes, simulating his checking for a draw play. If the offensive lineman pulls to either direction, the linebacker moves with the blocker while yelling "pull—pull—pull".

Coaching Points:

- A running back and a quarterback can be added after the linebacker has mastered the fundamental reactions to the various offensive lineman reads.

- This drill is most effective when a team's defensive philosophy is to have the inside linebackers key heavily on the offensive lineman.

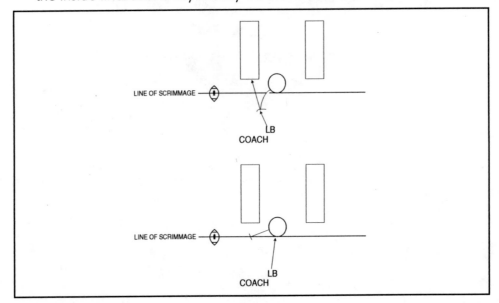

DRILL #57: RUSH AND CHASE

Objective: To enhance the defensive lineman's ability to react to a draw play after rushing the passer.

Equipment Needed: Two free-standing dummies; a football.

Description: The two free-standing dummies are positioned approximately five yards in front of the line of scrimmage. A defensive lineman aligns across a player designated as an offensive lineman. A quarterback and a running back are included in the drill. The running back is positioned approximately five yards behind the line of scrimmage. On the simulated snap, the defensive lineman rushes the passer as the offensive lineman simulates the first movement of a dropback pass block. The quarterback drops back and hands the ball off to the running back on a draw play. The defensive lineman should plant and retrace his path back to the line of scrimmage as soon as he recognizes the ball being handed off. The defensive lineman should yell "draw—draw—draw" as he plants and retraces his steps back to the line of scrimmage. The defensive lineman should sprint to the dummy and tag it.

Coaching Points:

- The quarterback should be directed to not hand off the ball to the running back and set up for a pass on various repetitions.

- If the quarterback doesn't hand off the ball to the running back, the defensive lineman should continue on his pass rush past the quarterback.

- The blocker can be activated as a live blocker to add a degree of difficulty to the drill.

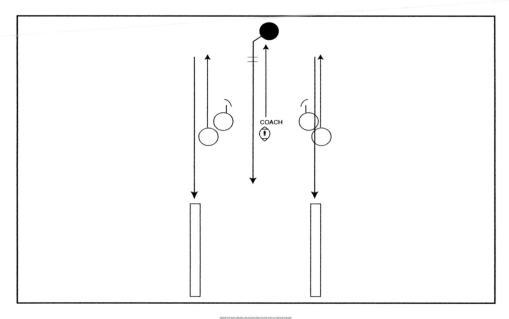

DRILL #58: DIAMOND MIRROR

Objective: To develop the defender's ability to backpedal and change direction in reaction to both a signal from the coach and the action of a man.

Equipment Needed: A football; four cones.

Description: The four cones are positioned five yards apart. The coach directs each player to assume his proper stance behind each cone by holding the football in front of his chest. With both hands on the ball, the coach extends his arms in front of his body. This action cues the players to backpedal in a straight line. After the players have backpedaled several yards, the coach moves the ball over his right shoulder. This cues the players to backpedal to their left at a 45-degree angle. The coach then moves the ball to a position over his left shoulder, cuing the players to backpedal to their right at a 45-degree angle. The process continues until the coach raises the ball straight over his head. The players respond by sprinting forward until the coach blows his whistle.

Coaching Points:

- The coach should direct the drill so that the front player isn't led to trip over the back cone.

- The players should attempt to stay an equal distance from each other.

- The coach can add variety to the drill by intentionally throwing an interception to one of the players; however, for safety reasons he should never throw the ball between two players.

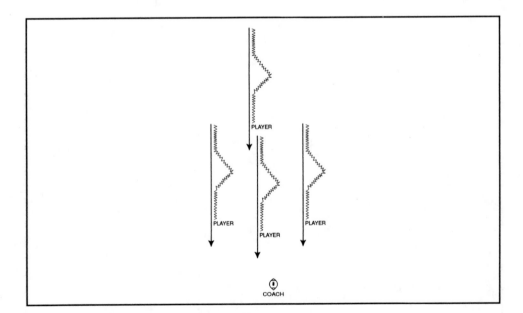

DRILL #59: WHAM AND ISO ATTACK

Objective: To enhance the ability of a linebacker to recognize an isolation play; to develop his technique in attacking the blocker.

Equipment Needed: A one-man sled.

Description: Two players are aligned side-by-side as offensive linemen. A one-man sled is placed two yards behind the gap between the offensive linemen, while a running back is positioned to the inside of the sled. A linebacker aligns approximately four yards from the line of scrimmage and assumes the proper stance. On the coach's command, the offensive linemen angle block to create a large gap between them. The lineman positioned on the inside of the tandem angles inside and the lineman positioned on the outside of the tandem angles outside. As the linemen angle block, the running back takes off to simulate a lead block on the linebacker. The linebacker takes his read step then fires straight ahead. The linebacker should pass up the lead blocker (since this drill does not involve live contact) and attack the sled with his inside shoulder. The linebacker should keep his outside arm free as he attacks the lead blocker on an isolation or wham play.

Coaching Points:

* The linebacker should drive through the sled until the coach blows a whistle.

* This drill is designed to teach the linebacker to instinctively attack the lead blocker and to not hesitate.

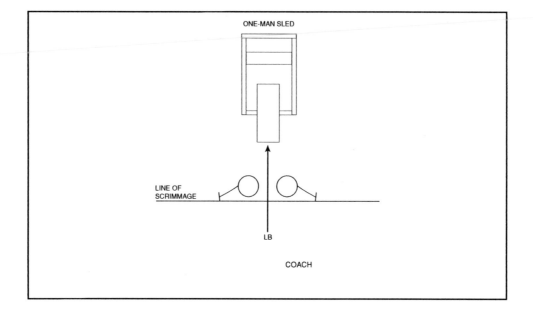

DRILL #60: BLOW UP THE IN

Objective: To improve the linebacker's ability to effectively read and counter a fullback quick trap.

Equipment Needed: Two low-profile bags; several cones.

Description: Two low-profile bags are placed parallel to each other. The bags are separated by a distance of five to six feet, with the ends facing the linebacker. Several cones are positioned on the ground to simulate offensive linemen. One cone is positioned in the backfield, four yards behind the center of the space between the bags. A player positions himself as a fullback in front of the backfield cone. On the coach's command the fullback takes two steps toward the gap between the bags. The linebacker, who is positioned in his normal alignment, should take a lateral step inside upon recognition of the fullback's angle. This lateral step to the inside is called the read step. The fullback returns to his starting point and the drill is repeated several times. Once the linebacker has practiced the inside read step in response to the fullback's inside path, the drill continues into the next phase. In the second phase, the fullback sprints to the space between the bags (i.e., the "IN") on the snap. The linebacker read steps and moves to meet him with his inside pad. No contact is necessary. In the third stage, an additional linebacker is added. On recognition of an "in" read, both linebackers read step and sprint to meet shoulder to shoulder in the gap between the bags.

Coaching Points:

- The linebackers should be in a ready position as they meet shoulder-to-shoulder in the gap.

- A quarterback should be added as the linebacker's read skills develop. A common trap read involves the quarterback showing his numbers (i.e., turning his back to the linebackers) to hand the ball off.

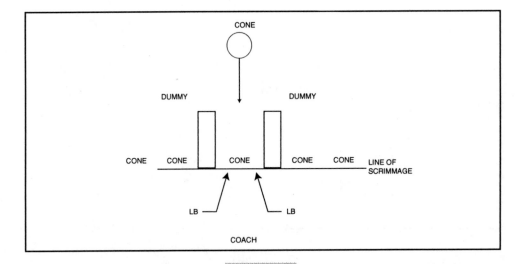

DRILL #61: SCRAPE TO THE AT

Objective: To improve the linebacker's ability to effectively read and react to a ball carrier attacking the off-tackle hole.

Equipment Needed: Four low-profile bags; several cones.

Description: Two low-profile bags are placed parallel to each other to designate the "IN" point (Note: The "IN" point is a reference point towards which the linebacker takes his initial step on the snap of the ball). A third bag and fourth bag are placed on a diagonal. The outside surface of the diagonal bags represent the "AT" point (Note: The "AT" point is a reference point that refers to the fullback's straight ahead point of attack). Cones are used to designate the remaining offensive line positions (e.g., guards and ends). On the coach's command, the fullback takes two steps toward the diagonal bag. The linebacker, who is positioned in his normal alignment, should take a lateral step outside upon recognition of the fullback's angle. This lateral step to the outside is called the read step. The fullback then returns to his starting point, and the drill is repeated several times. Once the linebacker has practiced the outside read step in response to the fullback's off-tackle path, the drill continues into the next phase. In the second phase, the fullback sprints to the "AT." The linebacker responds by read stepping to the outside and moving to fit with the running back. The linebacker should meet the running back with his outside shoulder free and with both shoulders square. This drill should not involve contact. As such, the players should stop on contact.

Coaching Points:

- If the linebackers normally flip their aligment, they should receive repetitions on each side of the ball.

- A read step is most effective when executed from an unusually tight base. This action keeps the linebacker from overextending his base on the read step.

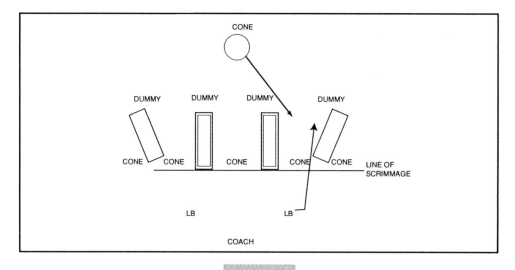

DRILL #62: SHUFFLE TO THE OUT

Objective: To improve the linebacker's ability to effectively read and react to a ball carrier running a wide play, such as a sweep or option.

Equipment Needed: Four low-profile bags; several cones.

Description: Two low-profile bags are placed parallel to each other to designate the "IN" point (Note: The "IN" is a reference point towards which the linebacker takes his first step on the snap of the ball.) A third bag and fourth bag are then placed on a diagonal. The outside surface of the diagonal bags represent the "OUT" point (Note: The "OUT" is a reference point towards which the linebacker should step when he recognizes the running back's outside angle.) Cones are used to designate the remaining offensive line positions (e.g., guards and tackles). On the coach's command the fullback takes two steps toward the outside, turning his shoulders perpendicular to the sideline. The linebacker, who is positioned in his normal alignment, should take a lateral step outside upon recognition of the fullback's angle. This lateral step to the outside is called the read step. The fullback returns to his starting point and the drill is repeated several times. Once the linebacker has practiced the outside read step in response to the fullback's off-tackle path, the drill continues into the next phase. In the second phase, the fullback sprints to the "OUT". The linebacker responds by read stepping to the outside and sprinting to the "OUT" demarcation. The linebacker should demonstrate an ability to make the tackle if the running back is forced back to the inside. No contact is needed in this drill; the players should stop on contact.

Coaching Points:

- The coach should be particularly alert for the linebacker bucket-stepping with his outside foot in response to an "OUT" read. A bucket-step is a backward step that causes the linebacker's hips and shoulders to open.

- A quick whistle should be used to prevent the running back from rounding the corner.

- This exercise is not a chase drill.

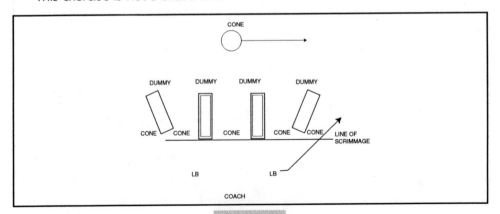

DRILL #63: SHUFFLE TO THE OTHER

Objective: To improve the linebacker's ability to effectively read flow to the side opposite his position.

Equipment Needed: Two low-profile bags; several cones.

Description: Two low-profile bags are placed parallel to each other. The bags are separated by a distance of five to six feet, with the ends facing the linebacker. Several cones are positioned on the ground to simulate offensive linemen. A player positions himself as a fullback in front of the backfield cone. On the coach's command the fullback takes two steps to an "OUT" angle (Note: Refer to Drill #62 for a description of the "OUT" reference point) in a directional flow away from the linebacker. The linebacker, who is positioned in his normal alignment, should take a lateral step inside upon recognition of the fullback's angle. This lateral step to the inside is called the read step. The fullback returns to his starting point and the drill is repeated several times. Once the linebacker has practiced the inside read step in response to the fullback's inside path, the drill continues into the next phase. In the next phase, the fullback sprints on an "OUT" angle away from the linebacker. The linebacker read steps and then shuffles to the playside "A" gap (i.e., first gap to the side of the back's path). As the linebacker shuffles, he gains some ground into the line of scrimmage and throws his eyes inside to check cutback and diagnose the center's blocking angle. The linebacker then sprints down the line on an inside-out angle to the running back. When a key read moves to the opposite side of the ball, the key read is called an "OTHER."

Coaching Point:

- The coach should check the linebacker to see if he is checking the "A" gap as he shuffles to pursue the back.

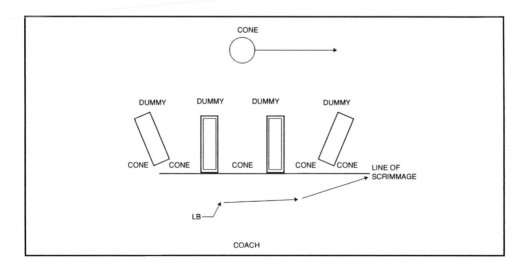

DRILL #64: FLASHING COLORS

Objective: To improve the linebacker's ability to effectively read and react to a counter or trap play.

Equipment Needed: Four low-profile bags; several cones.

Description: Two low-profile bags are placed parallel to each other to designate the "IN" reference point, as described in Drill #62. The bags are separated by a distance of five to six feet, with the ends facing the linebacker. Several cones are positioned on the ground to simulate offensive linemen. A player positions himself as a fullback in front of the backfield cone and a live guard is positioned in front of the linebacker. Cones are used to designate the remaining offensive line positions (e.g., tackles and ends). On the coach's command the fullback takes two steps toward the diagonal bag as the guard pivots and turns inside-showing his earhole to the linebacker, the linebacker, who is positioned in his normal alignment, should take a lateral step outside upon recognition of the fullback's angle. This lateral step to the outside is called the read step. The fullback and guard return to their starting point and the drill is repeated several times. Once the linebacker has practiced the outside read step in response to the fullback's off-tackle path, the drill continues into the next phase. In the second phase, the fullback sprints to the "AT" point (Note: Refer to Drill #61 for a description of the "AT" reference point), while the guard pulls to the opposite side of the ball. This combination is called a "flashing color" read. A flashing color read overrules the primary read of the back's attack angle. On the flashing color read, the linebacker plants off his read step and sprints to the playside. The guard should keep a low stance and not pop up as he reads the flashing color.

Coaching Points:

- When a linebacker gets an "earhole" read by the lineman going against the grain of the primary key, the read is a flashing color.

- The linebacker should yell "pull—pull—pull," as he plants and shuffles toward the path of the guard's pull.

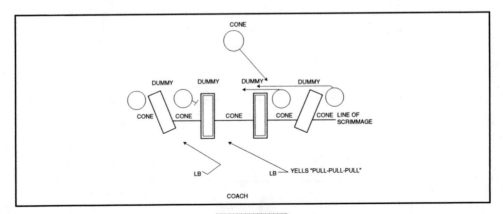

DRILL #65: OPEN - CLOSED DOOR

Objective: To improve the linebacker's ability to effectively read and react to an open-closed door read with a playside AT read.

Equipment Needed: Four low-profile bags; several cones.

Description: This drill involves a defensive lineman and a linebacker who plays over the guard. A coach plays quarterback and a running back is positioned four yards behind the coach. An offensive guard and an offensive tackle, are positioned on the line of scrimmage. The defensive lineman aligns in an outside shade on the offensive tackle while the linebacker aligns over the guard. On the coach's cadence, the running back runs an "AT" path (Note: Refer to Drill #61 for a description of the "AT" reference point) toward the guard's tail while the guard blocks inside. The offensive tackle also blocks inside in an attempt to seal the linebacker. The defensive lineman should squeeze the offensive tackle's down block and flatten his shoulders. The linebacker simultaneously read steps to the outside and reacts to attack the "AT." The linebacker should attack the "AT" to meet the running back with his outside arm free. When the defensive lineman closes in front of the linebacker, the linebacker sees the buttocks of the defensive lineman and the open door to the "AT" is closed. The linebacker should scrape outside and fit with his inside pad to the outside pad of the defensive tackle. If the tackle blocks the defensive lineman outward, the door is considered to be open. When the linebacker gets an open door read, he should attack the most dangerous threat on his path to the "AT" angle. With an open door read, the linebacker will normally face a base block by the guard or a lead blocker from the backfield.

Coaching Points:

- The linebacker should consider every door open until it is closed by the defensive lineman squeezing inside.

- An open-closed door read is an important skill for the defender and linebacker in the odd structured front.

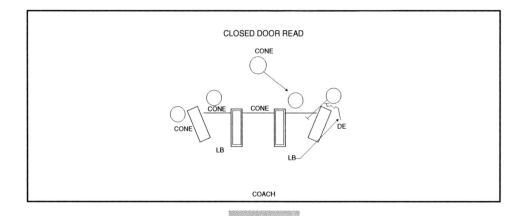

DRILL #66: UNCOVERED POP-UPS

Objective: To develop the ability of the zone coverage middle safety to read through the uncovered lineman.

Equipment Needed: A football; three cones.

Description: An offensive guard is positioned near a cone designating the center. Two cones are positioned approximately ten yards to the outside of the middle cone. The two outside cone designate the outside edge of the alley located to each side of the ball. The coach acts as the quarterback, while the safety aligns in his proper stance at the depth of twelve to fifteen yards. On the coach's command, the safety initiates his read steps and looks to the quarterback through the offensive guard. The offensive guard and the coach act together to give the middle safety various reads (e.g., run to the left, run to the right, dropback pass, play pass, sprint pass left, etc.). The free safety learns to use the guard as cheat mechanism and to not be fooled on play pass. The guard also gives the free safety a faster run key. When the guard shows a sweep to the left, the free safety sprints to the left cone. When the guard shows a run to the right, the safety sprints to the right cone.

Coaching Points:

- This drill is an excellent tool to teach and sharpen the uncovered "cheat" read of the offensive lineman.

- The middle zone safety should understand that even though an uncovered lineman may show a run read, he still is a "pass first" player.

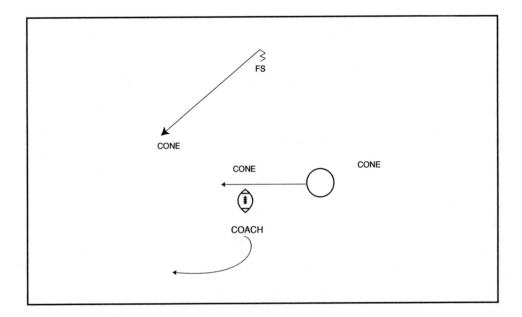

DRILL #67: QUICK DROP READS

Objective: To develop the ability of the zone coverage cornerback to read the quarterback on the three-step drop.

Equipment Needed: A football; two cones.

Description: This drill involves a defensive back and a wide receiver. The defensive back aligns in the cushion coverage position, approximately five yards off the receiver. The coach acts as the quarterback. On the coach's signal, the receiver takes off on a slant route or an out route. The coach shows the quick drop mechanics of a quarterback throwing a short-drop route. Short-drop quarterback mechanics include holding the hands high and exhibiting a high back shoulder. When the defensive back reads these characteristics, he should "sit down" and collision the wide receiver's route. The coach may throw the ball to the receiver or simply hold the ball while the defensive back covers the receiver's route. The drill may be stopped at any time by the coach blowing his whistle.

Coaching Points:

- The coach can run this drill live and occasionally mix in a five-step drops and routes once the defensive back demonstrates appropriate skill at reading the quick drop.

- The defensive back should use a "soft" catching technique with his hands as he collisions the receiver. He must not lose his balance and must be able to recover to cover the receiver deep.

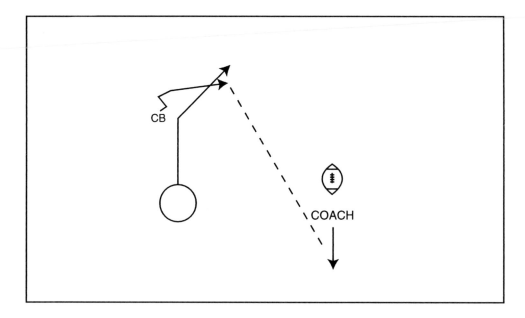

DRILL #68: DEEP DROP READS

Objective: To develop the ability of the zone coverage cornerback to read the quarterback on the five- and seven-step drop.

Equipment Needed: A football; two cones.

Description: This drill involves a defensive back and a wide receiver. The defensive back aligns in the cushion coverage position, approximately five yards off the receiver. The coach acts as the quarterback. On the coach's signal, the receiver takes off on a deep curl route or a go route. The coach shows the quick-drop mechanics of a quarterback throwing a intermediate or deep drop route. Five-and seven-step drop quarterback mechanics include holding the hands low on the drop and exhibiting a low back shoulder as the quarterback drives backward. When the defensive back reads these characteristics, he should play soft and be ready to flip his hips to cover the wide receiver's route. The coach may throw the ball to the receiver or simply hold the ball while the defensive back covers the receiver's route. The drill may be stopped at any time by the coach blowing his whistle.

Coaching Points:

- The coach may run this drill live and occasionally mix in a one- and three-step drops and routes once the defensive back demonstrates adequate skill at reading both types of quarterback drops, short and intermediate-to-long.

- The coach should emphasize the defensive back's backpedal technique and flip of the hips on a straight line.

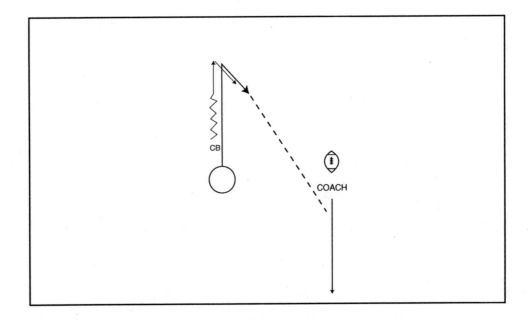

CHAPTER 8

TACKLING DRILLS

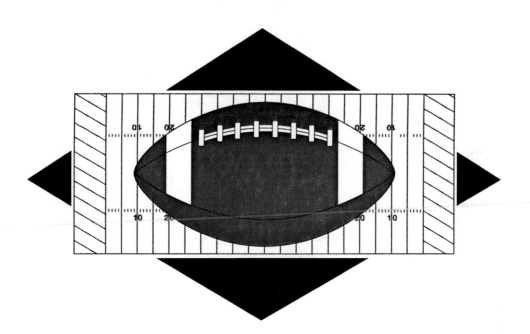

DRILL #69: FORM TACKLING

Objective: To develop the player's tackling technique.

Equipment Needed: A hand shield.

Description: Two players face each other from a distance of 4-5 feet away. The player designated as a ball carrier holds the hand shield with both hands so that the shield is held in front of his chest. The shield holder moves to his right at a slow and controlled pace. The tackler mirrors the movement of the shield holder, closing the distance to the shield holder. The tackler should maintain the proper tackling position as he closes to the shield holder. To maintain the proper tackling position, the tackler:

- *Keeps his eyes up.*

- *Keeps his neck bowed and his head back.*

- *Pulls his shoulders back so that his back is flat.*

- *Sets his feet shoulder width apart.*

- *Bends his knees and flexes his hips so that his back lowers to the desired angle.*

Coaching Points:

- The coach should not allow the tackler to drive the shield holder into the ground.

- The coach should strictly enforce the tackler's proper head positioning and not allow the tackler to hit with his head leading his shoulders.

- The drill is best done in the following sequence—walk through, half-speed, and three-quarters speed.

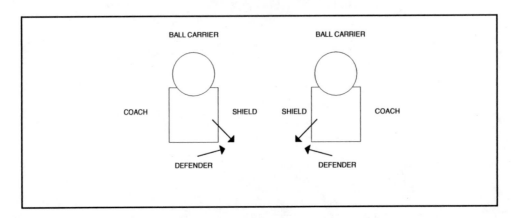

DRILL #70: FORM FIT

Objective: To teach the player the proper technique of a form tackle.

Equipment Needed: A hand shield.

Description: Two players face each other from a distance of two feet away. The player designated as a ball carrier holds the hand shield with both hands so that the shield is held in front of his chest. As shield holder steps forward, the tackler strikes the shield with proper technique. To maintain the proper tackling technique, the tackler should:

- *Keep his chin level.*
- *Keep his neck bowed and his head back.*
- *Pull his shoulders back so that his back is flat.*
- *Set his feet shoulder width apart.*
- *Bends his knees and flex his hips so that his back lowers to the desired angle.*

The tackler should strike the shield with his chest and the front of his shoulders. His helmet's facebar should make only a very slight contact on the shield as he strikes upward through the shield. The tackler should use both his arms to club upward under the shield holders armpits, raking the arms of the shield holder upward. The tackler should finish the club by clamping the arms around the shield holder. The tackler should bring his hands together as he hits "on a rise" through the shield holder. The tackler churns his legs and squeezes the shield holder as he drives the shield holder backward for several steps.

Coaching Points:

- The coach should not allow the tackler to drive the shield holder into the ground.
- The drill should never be done full speed.
- The tackler should focus his eyes on the target (i.e., he should pick out a spot on which to concentrate).

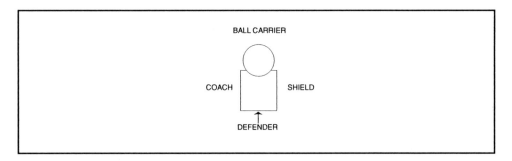

DRILL #71: MAT TACKLING

Objective: To develop the player's tackling form and give him a feel for driving a ball carrier to his back.

Equipment Needed: A hand shield; a large mat.

Description: Standing on the edge of a large mat, a player designated as a ball carrier holds the hand shield with both hands so that the shield is held in front of his chest. On the other edge of the mat, the defender aligns directly in front of the ball carrier and assumes the ready position with his feet moving. The ball carrier starts toward the defender, and the defender executes a form tackle on the ball carrier. Because of the safety factor of the large mat, the tackler may drive the ball carrier backward, driving him to his back. The ball carrier may also jog at a 45-degree angle to either side of the tackler, in which case, the tackler should may execute an angle tackle.

Coaching Points:

- The tackler should strike the hand shield with his shoulder pads.

- The coach should make sure that he tackler doesn't butt the shield with his helmet.

- The tackler should drive his legs and hit on the rise through the shield and ball carrier.

- As with most tackling drills, both players should be in full gear.

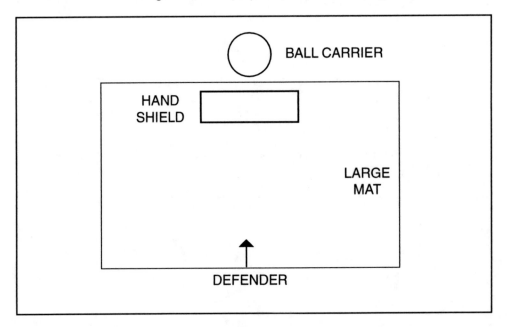

DRILL #72: HANGING BAG TACKLING

Objective: To develop the defender's ability to run through the tackle.

Equipment Needed: A hanging bag.

Description: The drill involves the use a hanging bag secured to a firmly set structure. A player faces the bag from approximately six feet away. On the coach's command, the player chaps his feet and attacks the dummy. The tackler should exhibit the proper tackling technique when contacting the dummy. As the dummy is driven backward to a position where it is suspended parallel to the ground, the tackler releases the dummy and continues forward. The tackler should get repetitions at running through the dummy using both the right and left shoulder as the primary contact surface.

Coaching Points:

- The coach should make sure the player has demonstrated proper tackling technique before being allowed to participate in this drill.

- The coach should emphasize hitting upward through the tackling dummy.

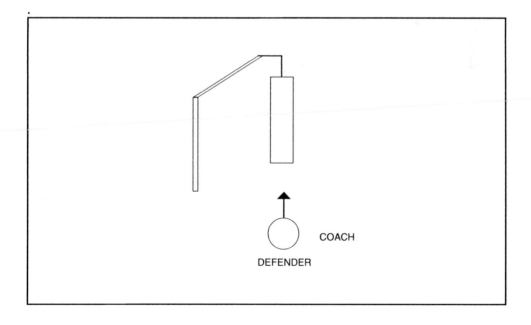

DRILL #73: MIRROR TACKLING

Objective: To emphasize agility and quickness when moving to tackle a ball carrier.

Equipment Needed: Two stand-up tackling dummies.

Description: Two players face each other from a distance of eight to ten yards away. One player is designated as a ball carrier while the other is designated as the tackler. Two stand-up dummies are positioned approximately ten yards apart on a line. On the coach's command, the ball carrier runs left and right several times. The tackler should mirror the ball carrier from a distance. On the coach's second command, the ball carrier will sprint to the outside of one of the dummies. The tackler must sprint to the tackling dummy and execute a driving tackle through the dummy from the proper angle.

Coaching Points:

- The tackler should maintain the proper relationship to the ball carrier during the mirror stage of the drill.

- The tackler should never cross his feet when mirroring the ball carrier.

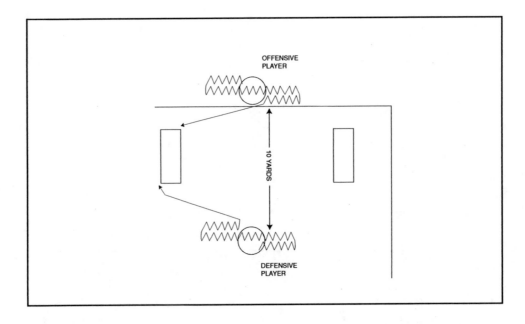

DRILL #74: DIAGONAL TACKLING

Objective: To enhance the defender's tackling form; to improve the defender's level of awareness of attacking the line of scrimmage.

Equipment Needed: A hand shield; five low-profile bags.

Description: A player designated as a ball carrier holds the hand shield with both hands so that the shield is held in front of his chest. The ball carrier is positioned approximately seven yards away from the tackler. Five low-profile bags are placed approximately three feet apart at a 45-degree angle, perpendicular to the line of scrimmage. The tackler positions himself flat on his back with head toward the ball carrier. On the coach's command, the tackler springs to his feet and shuffles over the bags to tackle the ball carrier. The ball carrier should jog to meet the tackler as he clears the last bag. The tackler should execute a form tackle on the ball carrier by striking the shield with the front of his chest and shoulders.

Coaching Points:

- The tackler should not strike the shield with his head.

- The coach should blow a quick whistle. The tackler should not be allowed to drive the ball carrier to the ground.

- The tackler should keep his feet moving and hit on the rise through the shield.

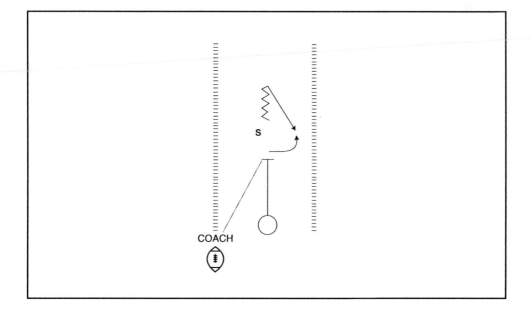

DRILL #75: SHUFFLE - TACKLE

Objective: To improve the defender's ability to focus on the ball carrier as he moves over obstacles.

Equipment Needed: Five low-profile bags or rolled-up towels; a football.

Description: Five bags are placed on the ground so that the player can work laterally over the bags. The row of bags should be set close enough together for the player to easily move laterally through the bags without having to overstride. A ball carrier is positioned in front of the first bag, approximately four yards away from the defender. The defender assumes a ready position and chops his feet. On the coach's command, the player moves laterally over the bags. He should maintain a good tackling demeanor (i.e., flat back, head up, hands low, etc.) as he shuffles over the bags. As the defender shuffles over the bags, the ball carrier jogs to the last bag in the row. The ball carrier should time his arrival at the last bag just as the defender exits the obstacle course. After the defender clears the last bag, he should execute a sharp form tackle on the ball carrier. The defender should execute an angle tackle on the ball carrier.

Coaching Points:

- If low-profile bags are unavailable, rolled-up towels may be used as the obstacle to step over.

- Several different lateral movement techniques can be used, including: a lead step technique a cross-over step technique; a two steps in the hole technique; and a two steps over and one step back technique.

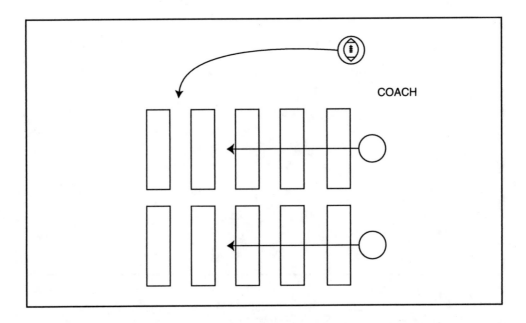

DRILL #76: ONE-MAN SLED TACKLING

Objective: To develop the tackler's technique of using his legs to drive through a ball carrier.

Equipment Needed: A one-man tackling sled.

Description: A tackler assumes the ready position approximately four feet from a one-man tackling sled. The tackler begins chopping his feet in place as he readies himself to attack the sled. The tackler attacks the sled with his face in the middle of the pad. He should continue running through the sled on contact, so that his feet don't die as he hits the pad. His face should make only slight contact with the pad as the front of the shoulders deliver a low-to-high blow through the pad of the sled. The coach sounds a whistle after the player has driven the sled a desired distance.

Coaching Points:

- The tackler should not strike the sled with his head. He should use the front of his shoulders.

- Younger players should use the top of either shoulder pad to strike the pad, alternating the right and left shoulder.

- Some one-man sleds are constructed to be twisted to the ground. The emphasis of tackling any type of one-man sled should be on the tackler running through the sled.

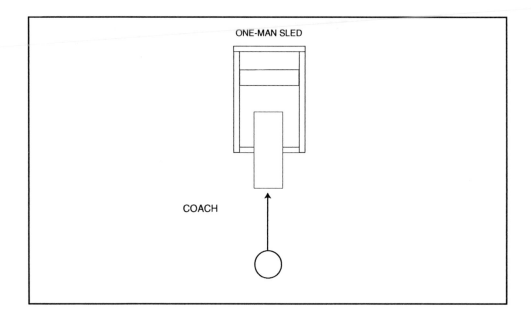

DRILL #77: TWO-MAN SLED TACKLING

Objective: To develop the tackler's technique of hitting a sled squarely with his shoulder pad.

Equipment Needed: A two-man tackling sled.

Description: Two tacklers assume the ready position approximately four feet from a two-man tackling sled. Both tacklers chop their feet in place. On the coach's command, each tackler should attack the sled with his inside shoulder striking the pad. Each player should strike the sled so that they lift the sled and "run with it". Both players must run through the sled on contact, so that their feet don't die as he hits the pad. Both players should bow their necks and keep their eyes looking upward while driving the sled. Both players may place their outside arm on the sled to balance themselves while they wrap their inside arm around the sled pad. The coach sounds a whistle after the player has driven the sled a desired distance.

Coaching Points:

- The coach should stand behind the sled so that he can see if the players keep their heads up.

- Each player should have a repetition with each shoulder contacting the pad.

- The defenders should focus on the target (i.e., the sled); they should pick out a spot on which to concentrate.

- The coach should attempt to have both players hit the sled at the same time.

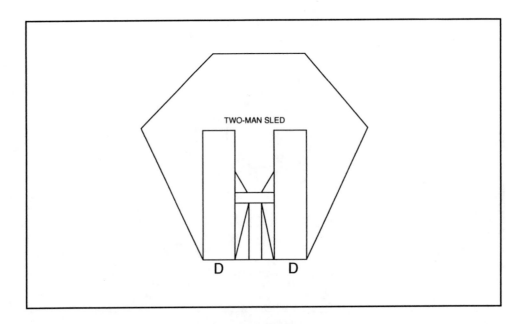

TWO-MAN SLED

D   D

DRILL #78: ANGLE TACKLING

Objective: To teach the player the proper technique of tackling from an angle.

Equipment Needed: A hand shield.

Description: Two players face each other from a distance of two feet away. The player designated as a ball carrier holds the hand shield with both hands so that the shield is held in front of his chest. The drill begins by having the coach direct the shield holder to step to his right. At that point, the tackler strikes the shield using proper techniques. If the shield holder steps to the left of the tackler, the defender should attack the shield with his right shoulder pad. The tackler should fit snuggly to the designated ball carrier and stay square to the ball carrier on contact. The tackler should wait to uncoil on the hand shield until the last possible moment, then strike an upward blow through the ball carrier. The tackler should drive the ball carrier backward for several steps. He shouldn't knock the ball carrier to the ground. This drill is a "daily must" for all positions.

Coaching Points:

- The tackler should get several repetitions with each shoulder.

- This drill—as all tackling drills—should be done in a controlled manner.

- The coach should position himself so that he can see if the tackler keeps his head up.

- Adhering to the proper techniques of tackling should be the primary emphasis of the drill.

- The defender should keep his eyes on the target (i.e., the hand shield); he should pick out a spot on which to concentrate.

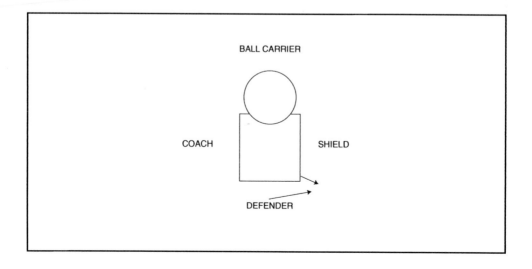

DRILL #79: THE BARREL

Objective: To develop the fundamentals of angle tackling.

Equipment Needed: A barrel, two cones, and several footballs.

Description: The barrel is positioned so that a line of players face each side. One line of players simulates the ball carrier while the other line of players assume the role of a defensive player. The front player of each line is positioned approximately five yards from the barrel. On the coach's command, the defensive player moves toward the barrel and chops his feet in place. The ball carrier sprints toward the barrel then breaks to one side. The defender should remain in the ready position until the ball carrier makes his cut. The defender should tackle the ball carrier "across the bow." A defender should use his shoulder to strike a blow on the ball carrier. This drill is designed for linebackers and defensive backs.

Coaching Points:

- This drill should be run a slow controlled pace—approximately half speed.

- The ball carrier should switch the ball to his outside arm as he cuts.

- The tackler should keep his head up as he puts his head across the bow. He should not use his head to make contact with the ball carrier.

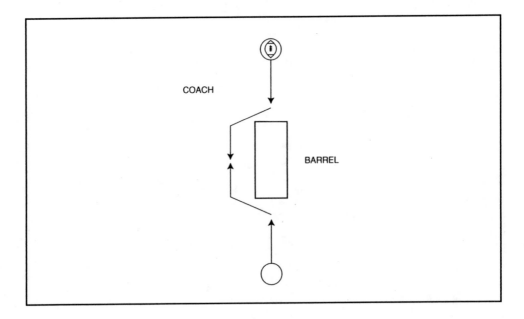

DRILL #80: SHUFFLE-BACK-TACKLE

Objective: To develop the defender's ability to react to a ball carrier making a cutback.

Equipment Needed: Three low-profile bags; one form tackling dummy.

Description: Three low-profile are positioned on the ground approximately 18 inches apart. The tackling dummy is positioned six to seven yards from the first dummy. A player assumes the ready position and begins to shuffle over the bags. A running back positioned approximately five yards away from the bags moves toward the defender's lead shoulder. As the defender shuffles over the second bag, the ball carrier cuts back toward the first bag. After the player reads the cut-back, he should immediately plant his lead foot and push off to accelerate to make a half-speed form tackle.

Coaching Points:

- The coach should encourage the players to look at him and stay low as they shuffle through the bags.

- Folded towels may be used in place of low-profile bags.

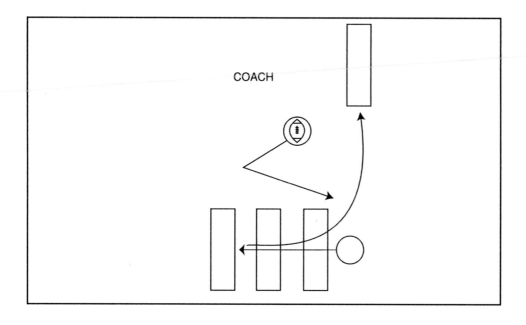

DRILL #81: CUSHION TACKLING

Objective: To develop the player's confidence in his ability to make a sure tackle from a big cushion.

Equipment Needed: A football.

Description: The coach stands on the hash mark and acts as a quarterback. A receiver is positioned in the middle of the field. A defensive back is positioned seven yards from the receiver. The defensive back backpedals as the receiver takes off. His objective is to keep a five yard cushion on the receiver. On the coach's command, the receiver runs a hitch route and the coach passes the ball to the receiver. The receiver can make a move in any direction after he catches the ball. The defender should break out of his backpedal to execute a high form tackle on the receiver. The coach should sound a quick whistle in this drill.

Coaching Points:

- When introducing this drill, the receiver's area should be restricted.

- The coach should control the drill so that the defensive back is able to experience success.

- The defensive back should tackle high and drive his legs until the coach sounds the whistle.

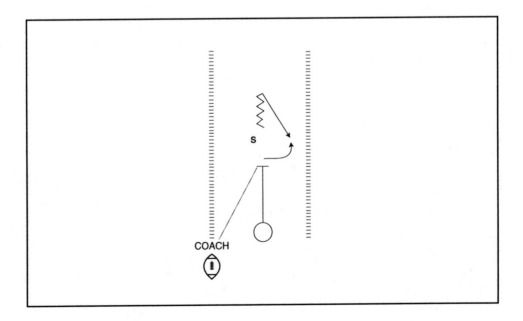

DRILL #82: SHED TACKLING

Objective: To develop the player's ability to shed a blocker and move to make a tackle.

Equipment Needed: A hand shield; a sled.

Description: A player designated as a ball carrier holds the hand shield with both hands so that the shield is held in front of his chest. The ball carrier is positioned behind a sled. The defensive player assumes his stance in front of the sled. On the coach's command, the defender attacks the sled using the proper technique. After delivering a blow to the sled, the defender moves to form tackle the ball carrier. The ball carrier should be moving to one side of the sled in a slow, controlled manner. The tackler executes a form tackle on the ball carrier and drives the ball carrier backward for several steps. The tackler should strike the ball carrier with an upward blow. The feet of the tackler should never stop moving.

Coaching Points:

- The coach should blow a quick whistle on this drill.

- The tackler should not put the ball carrier on the ground.

- The blow to the sled should be a sharp, explosive strike.

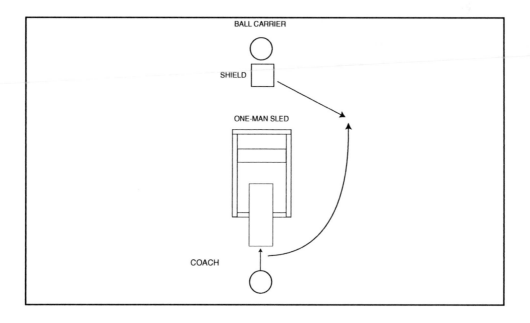

DRILL #83: OPEN FIELD TACKLING

Objective: To develop the defender's confidence in his ability to make an open field tackle.

Equipment Needed: Six cigar-shaped dummies or six cones.

Description: Three dummies are placed along a ten-yard line on the field. The second set of three dummies are placed five yards across from the first set. The dummies are arranged to make three separate tackling stations. A defensive player aligns midway between each pair of dummies. A ball carrier is positioned four yards from the front player. On the coach's command, the ball carrier moves toward the first tackler. The ball carrier is allowed to make only one move on the defender. The defender should chop his feet and assume a good hitting position as the ball carrier approaches. Once the ball carrier makes his move and gets within tackling distance, the defender should execute a high form tackle on the ball carrier. The coach should blow a quick whistle. After the first defender gets his opportunity to tackle the ball carrier, the second defender breaks down to ready himself for the ball carrier. The drill continues in the same manner until each defender executes a form tackle on the ball carrier. This drill is designed for linebackers and defensive backs.

Coaching Points:

- The coach should make sure the player has demonstrated proper tackling technique before being allowed to participate in this drill.

- If the tackler fails to successfully tackle the ball carrier, he should stay in to tackle the next ball carrier. He should not be allowed more than three consecutive opportunities.

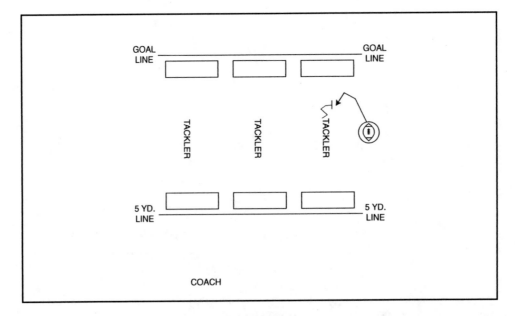

DRILL #84: BOUNDARY TACKLING

Objective: To teach a player how to utilize the sideline when moving to tackle a ball carrier.

Equipment Needed: A football.

Description: A ball carrier is positioned near the numbers of the field, approximately nine yardsfrom the sideline. The defender aligns one yard inside of the ball carrier and moves toward the ball carrier on an inside-out angle. The defender should force the ball carrier to the sideline while preventing a cut back. The tackler should square his shoulders to the ball carrier and tackle the ball carrier above the waist.

Coaching Points:

- The tackler should keep his body under control and execute a high tackle on the ball carrier.

- The tackler should not attempt to bring the ball carrier to the ground. He should use his legs to drive the ball carrier out of bounds.

- This drill is designed for perimeter players such as outside linebackers and defensive backs.

- The defender should focus his eyes on the target (i.e., he should pick out a spot on which to concentrate).

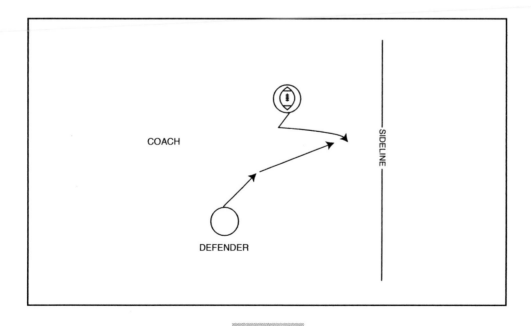

DRILL #85: BLIND TACKLING

Objective: To develop the player's ability to react and orient himself to make a sure form tackle.

Equipment Needed: A football; five low-profile footwork bags or folded towels.

Description: Five low-profile footwork bags are positioned approximately two feet apart. This drill involves two players, one player acting as a ball carrier and one player acting as a tackler. One player lies with his head at one end of the bag while the other player lies with his head at the other end of the bag. On the coach's command, the players get up off the ground. The ball carrier runs through one of the spaces between the bags as the tackler moves to execute a "run through" form tackle on the ball carrier. The tackler should tackle high but still strike an upward blow through the ball carrier's chest. The coach should sound a quick whistle as the tackler demonstrates the proper technique of running through the ball carrier.

Coaching Points:

- This drill should be done at half-speed.

- The emphasis of this drill should be on the tackler demonstrating rapid acceleration of his feet as he contacts the ball carrier. Stopping the feet on contact is a major cause of poor tackling technique.

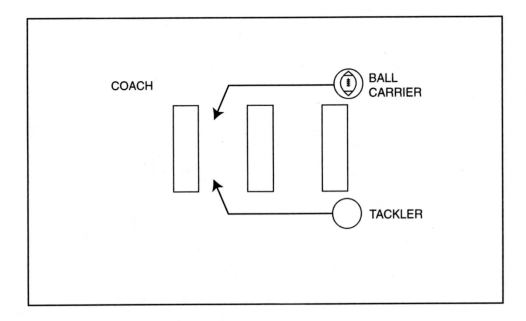

DRILL #86: PUSH HIM BACK

Objective: To improve the defender's ability to contact a ball carrier without overextending.

Equipment Needed: A football; four low-profile footwork bags

Description: Four or more low-profile footwork bags are placed on the ground parallel to each other. Two players align at the first bag facing each other. One player is designated as a ball carrier, while the other player is designated as a tackler. On the coach's command, the ball carrier runs under control in the first "hole" (i.e., the space between the first and second bag). The tackler reacts by shuffling into the hole and shooting his hands into the ball carrier. The tackler should use his hands to jam the ball carrier and knock him back. After the intial contact, the ball carrier rebounds and then moves into the next hole as the tackler shuffles to meet him. On the last repetition, the defender pushes the ball carrier back beyond the bag.

Coaching Points:

- Special emphasis should be placed on the tackler's body technique. The tackler should keep head back, his buttocks low, his lower back arched, and his feet continually moving.

- This drill is an excellent "noncontact" tackling exercise that can enable a coach to teach the defender the proper body position when tackling.

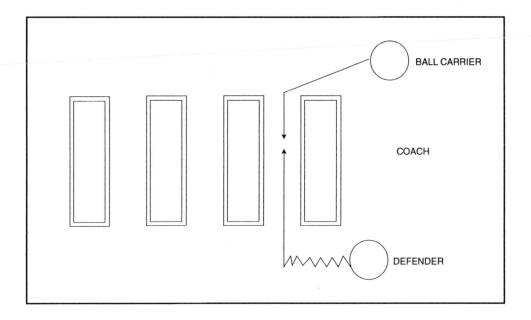

DRILL #87: SHOULDER ROLL TACKLING

Objective: To teach defenders to recover from being knocked down, get up and quickly become oriented and make the tackle.

Equipment Needed: A football; two cones.

Description: The drill involves two player—each approximately two yards away from a yard line. One player acts as a ball carrier, while the other is a tackler. The players start the drill approximately eight yards apart, equidistant between two cones set five yards apart. Both players are in an upright position, facing in the same direction. The defender is facing the back of the ball carrier. On command from the coach, the ball carrier turns around toward the defender, catches the football tossed to him by the coach, and then attempts to sprint through the two cones. Simultaneously, the defender does a shoulder roll, immediately comes up into a fundamental hitting position, and tackles the ball carrier.

Coaching Points:

- The proper techniques and fundamentals of tackling should be emphasized.

- Variety can be added to the drill by having the coach wait until the defender comes to his feet after his shoulder roll before he tosses the ball to the ball carrier.

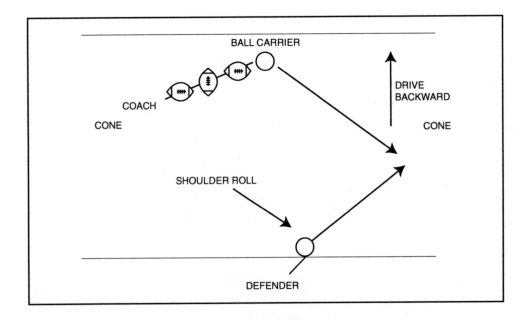

DRILL #88: ALLEY TACKLING

Objective: To teach the free safety to fill the alley and break down to make the tackle on the ball carrier.

Equipment Needed: A football; eight cones.

Description: Four cones form an alley on each side of the ball. The coach acts as the quarterback. A running back is positioned so that he can move to receive a sweep pitch to either side. The safety aligns at the appropriate depth and position. On the simulated snap, the coach reverses out and tosses the ball to the running back. The free safety takes his recognition steps and reacts to the toss. The running back secures the toss and hits the alley as the free safety attacks the line of scrimmage while keeping an inside-out angle to the ball carrier. The objective of the free safety is to make a headup form tackle or an angle tackle on the ball carrier. The type of tackle the free safety makes is related to his speed in getting lo the alley. If the safety is tardy in his arrival to the alley, he is forced to use an angle tackling technique. Whatever the tackling technique, the safety must not allow the ball carrier to cut back cleanly.

Coaching Points:

- If the free safety gets into the alley early enough, he should break down with his shoulders square to the line of scrimmage.

- The free safety should concentrate on tackling high with a proper tackling technique.

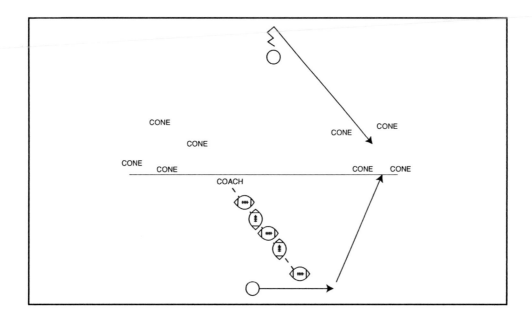

DRILL #89: TACKLE AND PURSUIT

Objective: To develop the player's tackling technique and practice the proper fundamentals of pursuit.

Equipment Needed: Two hand shields; six cones.

Description: Two players are designated as a ball carriers, while one serves as a defender. They each hold a hand shield with both hands so that the shield is held in front of their chest. Three cones are placed in an equilateral triangle on each side of the ball carriers. The defender assumes the ready position approximately two feet from ball carrier "A". On the coach's signal, ball carrier "A" steps forward, and the defender executes a form tackle. The defender follows through on the tackle, as the coach blows his whistle. When the coach blows his whistle, again the defender releases ball carrier "A" and pursues ball carrier "B." Ball carrier "B" begins running in a controlled pace around the triangle where he and the tackler will cross paths. The defender should then make a form tackle on ball carrier "A".

Coaching Points:

- As with all instructional tackling drills, this drill should be done at a slow, contolled pace.

- The coach should emphasize that the defender should drive through the tackle and not let his feet die on contact with ball carrier "B".

- The defender should never drive the ball carrier into the ground.

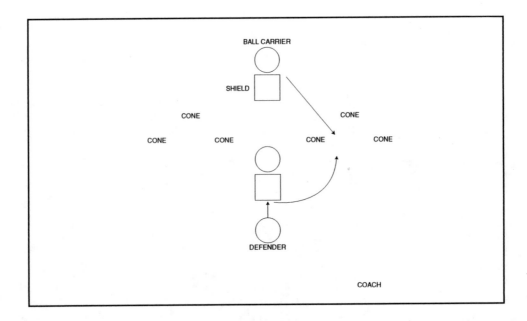

DRILL #90: TWO-MINUTE TACKLING

Objective: To develop the ability of the defensive player to tackle the ball carrier inside the boundary before he gets out of bounds to stop the clock.

Equipment Needed: A football.

Description: This drill involves a ball carrier and a tackler. The players are positioned near the numbers of the field approximately fifteen yards apart. The ball carrier can be positioned inside the numbers to make the drill easier for the tackler. On the coach's command, the ball carrier attempts to run out of bounds. The tackler reacts to the ball carrier's movement and attempts to execute a high tackle on the ball carrier before he gets to the sideline.

Coaching Points:

- The tackler should attempt to hold up the ball carrier so that his teammates can arrive and possibly strip the football away.

- The ball carrier should not be tackled to the ground. A quick whistle should control this drill.

- The coach should maintain tight control over this drill with a quick whistle.

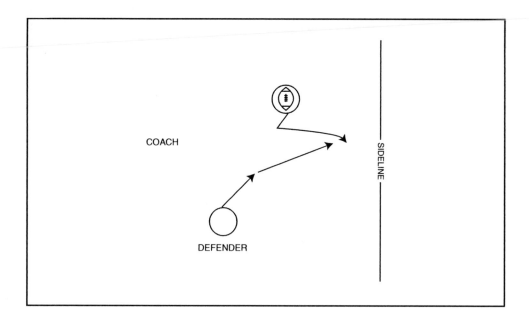

DRILL #91: MACHINE GUN

Objective: To develop the ability of a defender to successfully take on a series of blockers, find the football, and execute proper form tackling.

Equipment Needed: A football.

Description: The coach aligns three blockers three yards apart, with the ball carrier three yards behind them. The coach has the defender face the offensive players from three yards away. On the coach's command, the defender attempts to engage and disengage each blocker. After disengaging the last blocker, the defender should form tackle the ball carrier.

Coaching Points:

- The defender should maintain proper balance and body control at all times during the drill.

- The defender should keep his knees bent and his feet moving as he encounters each blocker.

- When tackling the ball carrier, the defender should employ proper form tackling techniques.

CHAPTER 9

SUDDEN CHANGE DRILLS

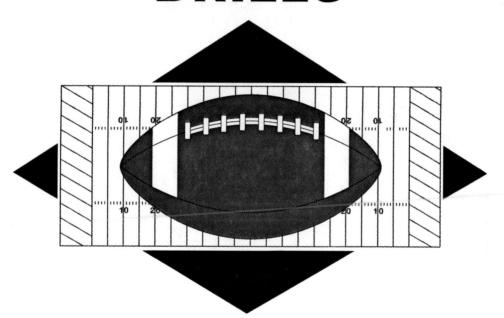

DRILL #92: FUMBLE RECOVERY

Objective: To teach players the proper method of recovering a fumble.

Equipment Needed: A football.

Description: A ball is placed three to four yards in front of a defender. On command, the defensive back dives forward to one hip and reaches out to the ball. Upon contacting the ground, the defender pulls the ball to his stomach. The defender should curl his knees to his stomach as he secures the ball close to his stomach. He should remain on his side and attempt to curl himself into a tight ball.

Coaching Points:

- The player should recover a fumble by sliding in the manner similar to a baseball player going into a base feet first.

- A player should never dive on top of a football to recover a fumble.

- A player should not roll on to his back, he should also not curl up in a way as to turn his back to an on-rushing opponent who is likely to dive for the ball.

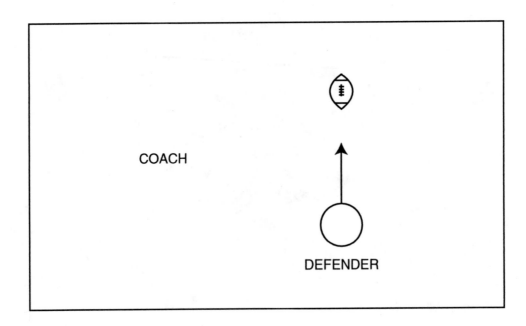

DRILL #93: STRIP THE BALL

Objective: To develop the ability of a defender to properly strip the football from a ball carrier.

Equipment Needed: A football.

Description: The coach instructs a ball carrier to put the football in a locked position under his arm. A defensive lineman then assumes a standing position behind the ball carrier. On the coach's command of "Fit!", the defender takes his hand to the ball and cups the point of it. He then takes his other hand and wraps it over the opposite shoulder of the ball carrier and grabs his jersey to ensure the tackle. On the coach's command of "Strip!", the defender pulls the football back toward him, stripping the ball out.

Coaching Points:

- The defender should make sure his hand is under the point of the football.

- The coach should emphasize to his defensive players that the most important aspect of this drill is that the defender ensure that he tackle the ball carrier by using both his off hand and his off arm.

- The effort to strip the ball out should be intense.

- Variety can be added to the drill by having both the defender and the ball carrier attempt to recover the ball once it has been stripped.

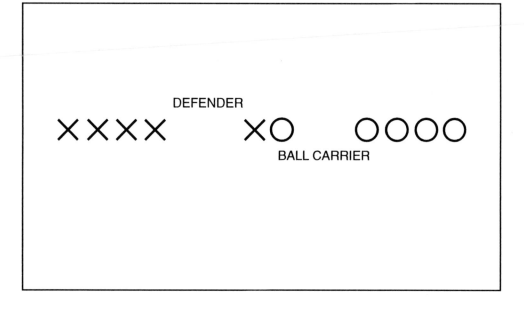

DRILL #94: ON-THE-GO FUMBLE RECOVERY

Objective: To improve the ability of the defensive lineman to change direction quickly and properly; to teach a defender to bounce up off the ground after being knocked down and to recover a fumble.

Equipment Needed: Six agility bags; a football.

Description: The coach should give a "Feet" command, which tells the defensive lineman his feet should be live and chopping in one spot. On the coach's signal, the defensive lineman should move laterally with his outside foot, changing direction over the bags. Once the coach sends the defensive lineman over the last bag, the coach throws the ball on the ground to the defender's right. The lineman should perform a seat roll and recover the fumble.

Coaching Points:

- The defensive lineman should remain in the proper football position throughout the entire drill.

- The defensive lineman should not use a cross over step to go over the bags. He should change directions as quickly as he can while maintaining good arm action.

- When the defensive lineman executes his seat roll, he should bounce up off the ground, using his hands to help him get up.

- When the defensive lineman recovers the fumbled football, he should grab it with two hands, pulling it in and seating it into his midsection with his chin tucked and his top leg protecting the football. The defensive lineman should end up in a fetal position, with a firm lock on the football.

- The defensive lineman should not jump, roll, or dive on top of the football.

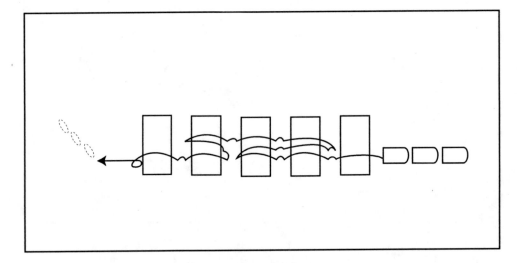

DRILL #95: PILE FIGHTER

Objective: To teach players to fight to gain possession of the ball in a pileup.

Equipment Needed: A medicine ball.

Description: Four to five players form a circle. Each player kneels so they are positioned immediately next to his teammate. Each player places his hands on his thighs as they kneel around a medicine ball placed in the middle of the circle. On the coach's command, the players attempt secure the medicine ball and pull it away from the rest of the teammates. The first player to gain sole possession of the medicine ball is the winner. The time limit is ten seconds to gain sole possession.

Coaching Points:

- The players should be positioned close together so that none of them hit heads.

- For competitive purposes, the players may be divided into teams of two.

- A football can be substituted for a medicine ball. The general rule, however, is the smaller the ball, the less competition in fighting for the ball. The first person to secure the ball normally keeps the smaller ball.

- This drill can be conducted without pads on a large padded mat.

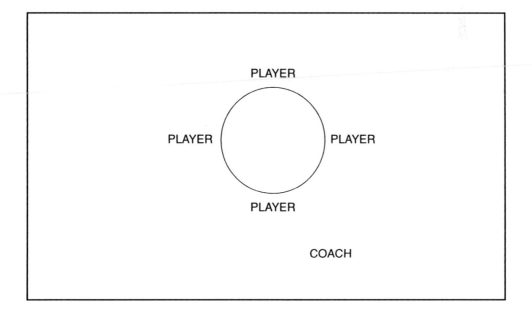

DRILL #96: SLED ATTACK AND FUMBLE RECOVERY

Objective: To develop the defensive lineman's ability to attack, then react to properly recover a fumble.

Equipment: A football; a two-man sled.

Description: A coach stands behind the two-man sled and holds a football in each hand. Two defensive lineman align in their proper three-point stance, approximately 18 inches away from the pad of the sled. Another coach, a manager, or a player is used to snap the ball on the coach's command (cadence), so the coach is able to stand back from the drill and observe the hand placement, elbow angle, and hip snap of the defenders. On movement, the defenders violently throw their hands into the pads with a following hip extension and drive the sled in a quick burst of churning footwork. Both players execute an outward seat roll and get up to recover a fumble as the coach rolls a ball out to both sides of the sled. The defensive linemen may alternate scooping up a fumble or recovering the fumble on the ground.

Coaching Points:

- The sled should fly upward and outward. No player or coach should stand on the sled; the sled should be kept as light as possible to increase the psychological benefit of the sled being knocked up into the air.

- This drill is a good exercise for linebackers, as well as defensive linemen.

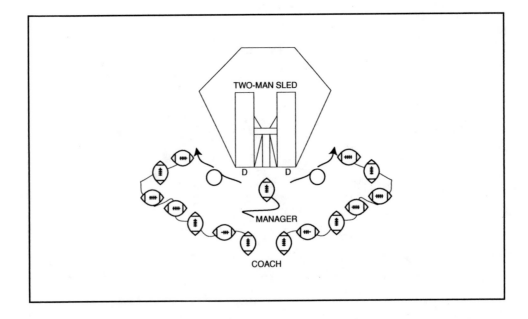

DRILL #97: FUMBLE SCOOPING

Objective: To teach players the proper method of scooping up a fumble to score.

Equipment Needed: Two footballs.

Description: Two players are positioned face to face. One player holds a football loosely in his hands while the second player assumes the ready position for a form tackle. The coach stands behind the ball carrier and holds a second football in his hand. The third player aligns five yards behind the form tackler. On the coach's command, the form tackler executes a form tackle on the ball carrier. At the same moment, the coach throws a bouncing football to the ground near the form tackler. The third defender comes up to scoop the fumble from the ground. The form tackler disengages from the form tackle after his second step of following through on the tackle. After the fumble is recovered by the third player, the players rotate and assume a new role. The ball carrier and the form tackler are included to give the fumble recovery drill a closer simulation of game conditions. The coach shouldn't simply toss the ball on the ground because, depending upon the rules governing play, a player may or may not be allowed to advance a recovered pitch out to the ground   (Note: The rules for interscholastic, intercollegiate and professional levels vary with regard to whether a fumble can be advanced). Including the form tackler and ball carrier provide a better simulation of the rule book definition of an advanceable fumble.

Coaching Point:

- When scooping a football, a player should turn his palms forward and point his extended fingers downward. Positioning his hands in this manner not only helps him recover the ball, it normally results in the ball being knocked toward the opponent's goal line should the recovery be muffed.

- A player should widen his stance as he approaches the ball. This action allows him to bend his knees and recover the fumble.

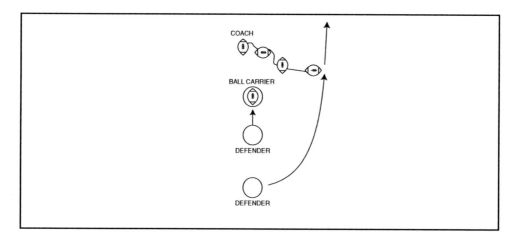

DRILL #98: BLOCK AND SCOOP

Objective: To train players to attempt to scoop up a blocked kick.

Equipment: Several footballs; a kicking tee; several flat shields.

Description: A kicker sets the ball on the kicking tee and places several flat shields in front and on both sides of the ball. A designated kick blocker sprints to block the kick, while four to five players rush the kick and sprint to scoop up the block. The coach stands behind and to the side of the kicker and holds a second football. If the designated kick blocker fails to block the kick, the coach throws a ball to the ground to simulate the blocked kick. A line of designated kick blockers should rotate in the drill. This drill is designed to teach a defensive player to instinctively scoop up a blocked kick.

Coaching Point:

- The defenders should scoop the ball, not fall on it.

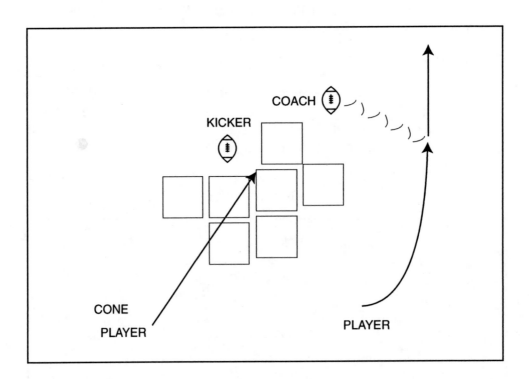

DRILL #99: PAINT STRIPPER

Objective: To develop the player's ability to strip the football from behind a ball carrier as he breaks away to score.

Equipment Needed: A football; two cones.

Description: Two cones are set up approximately ten yards apart. Two players start at one cone with one player standing behind the other. The front player carries the football in his right hand. The player in front begins to jog toward the second cone. The second player allows the ball carrier to get seven yard lead on him, then takes off to catch him. When the second player closes to within striking distance, he uses his left arm to reach over the top of the ball carrier's left shoulder and grab cloth. The tackler then violently swings his right arm downward and secures a grip on the nose of the football. He then instantaneously jerks upward on the nose of the football, ripping it from the ball carrier's grasp. The ball carrier and the tackler then switch roles at the next cone and return to the starting point. The drill continues with each player getting numerous repetitions at stripping the ball carrier before he gets to the next cone. A player knows to attempt to strip a player when he is closing to the ball carrier after he has broken free on his way to the paint (i.e. painted grass in the endzone).

Coaching Point:

- Several stripping techniques can be used. For example, another effective technique is the uppercut punch to the football from behind.

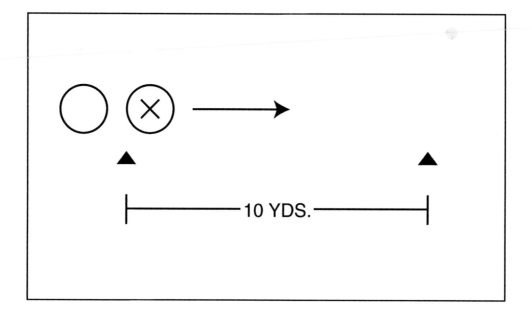

DRILL #100: BACK-TO-BACK STRIP

Objective: To improve the ability of a defensive back or linebacker to come around the receiver who has already caught the ball and strip it out of his hands.

Equipment: A football.

Description: Two players are positioned back-to-back. A coach stands facing one of the players from a point approximately fifteen yards away. The coach passes the ball to the player whom he is facing. The player catching the ball acts as a receiver while the player immediately behind him acts as the defender. The defender reacts to the sound of the ball hitting the receiver's hands and immediately runs around and attempts to strip the ball from the receiver. The defender should try to strip the ball by jerking one or both of the receiver's arms downward. Each player should get several repetitions as both a receiver and a defender.

Coaching Points:

- The defender should be in a ready position with his buttocks touching the tail of the receiver.

- The defender should use his arms to keep contact with the receiver.

- The defender must be prepared to tackle the defender in case the effort to strip the ball from the receiver's hands is unsuccessful.

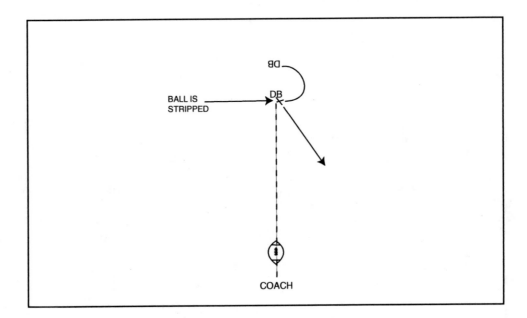

DRILL #101: BLOCK THAT KICK

Objective: To teach players the proper angle and how to lay out to block a kick.

Equipment Needed: A large padded mat; a football.

Description: The drill involves positioning a player approximately eight yards away from a large mat. The coach stands at the edge of the mat holding a football. Tape can be used to mark a large rectangle on the mat where the ball would be contacted by a kicker standing in the coach's position. On a movement cue of a simulated snap, the defender sprints to dive into the rectangular area on the mat. The blocker should cross his arms at the wrists and keep his eyes open to watch the ball hit his hands or arms. He should land on his side when he hits the mat. After several dry runs, the player can practice with the coach actually kicking the ball.

Coaching Points:

- The coach should direct the drill with the player's success as the central issue. Athletes who develop confidence in their kick-blocking abilities often block more kicks than their teammates, regardless of speed and talent.

- Every player on the defense should be instructed on the proper technique of breaking free and blocking a kick.

- Linemen who do not immediately break free through the line of scrimmage should use their pass rushing technique and jump straight up or get a hand up in an attempt to block the kick.

- When the defender breaks free from the blockers, he should aim for the spot when the ball comes off the kicker's foot.

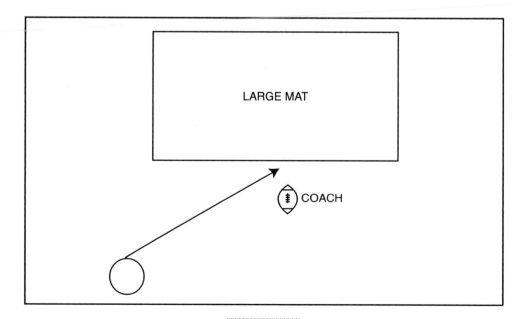

LARGE MAT

COACH

ABOUT
THE AUTHORS

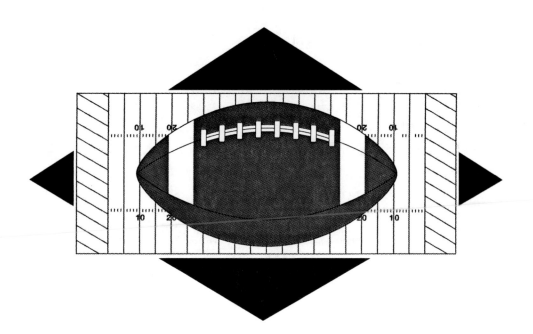

BILL ARNSPARGER

Bill Arnsparger retired in February 1995, after 45 years in collegiate and professional athletics, including five years in athletic administration. Arnsparger began his coaching career at his alma mater, Miami of Ohio, in 1950. He then served as an assistant at Ohio State under Woody Hayes, at Kentucky under Blayton Collier, and at Tulane under Tommy O'Boyle. Blanton Collier was also Bill's high school coach at Paris (KY) High School.

Arnsparger began his NFL career in 1964, when he joined Don Shula's staff with the Baltimore Colts where he coached until 1970. In 1970, Arnsparger followed Shula to Miami, and remained there as defensive coordinator until he became the head coach of the New York Giants in 1974, a post he held until mid-way through the 1976 season when he rejoined Shula in Miami.

As defensive coordinator and assistant head coach, Arnsparger was the architect of the Dolphin's No-Name Defense in the early 1970's that contributed to three Super Bowls (VI, VII, VIII), and two back-to-back Super Bowl wins (VII, VIII), including the undefeated 17-0 season in 1972 and the 15-2 record in 1973. He later developed the "Killer B's" defense in the early 80's that was a part of the Dolphins fourth Super Bowl appearance (XVII). His defenses ranked first or second in the NFL for the fewest points allowed in nine of his eleven seasons with Miami. In 1983, his final year with the Dolphins, Miami allowed an NFL-low 15.6 points a game.

In 1984, Arnsparger left the NFL to become head football coach at LSU. He guided the Tigers to a conference championship in 1986, two Sugar Bowl appearances, a Liberty Bowl berth, and was named SEC Coach of the Year in 1984 and 1986.

In 1987, he joined the University of Florida as Director of Athletics. During his five years (1987-'91) at the helm of the Gators' athletic program Arnsparger's leadership placed a premium on academics as well as athletics. Between 1989-'91, UF student athletes earned the most all-academic honors for a three-year total in school history. Florida's combined men's and women's programs ranked among the ten most successful in the nation of each of Arnsparger's years according to *USA Today*. He left the University after his fifth year, to return to the sideline, where he joined Bobby Ross as a member of the Chargers' staff.

His tenure as defensive coordinator with San Diego was equally as successful. In 1992, the Chargers' defense ranked 2nd in the AFC and 4th in the NFL, and led the AFC in rushing defense. It was the team's highest overall defensive ranking since the AFL-NFL merger in 1970. In 1993, they were even better, allowing a league-low 3.2 yards per rush, and just 82.1 yards rushing a game to rank 2nd in the NFL. 1994 was a banner year for the Chargers, with the San Diego defense making a key fourth-down play in the closing seconds of the AFC championship game to propel the Chargers to their first Super Bowl (XXIX). In his three years as San Diego's defensive coordinator, the Chargers allowed only two 100-yard rushers in 53 games, including allowing none in 30 consecutive games.

Bill was born December 16, 1926, in Paris, Kentucky. After service in the U. S. Marine Corps, he entered Miami University in Oxford, Ohio, where he obtained a BS degree in education and a M.Ed. in school administration. As a player at Miami, he played under three coaches: Sid Gilliam, George Blackburn, and Woody Hayes. He has coached in six Super Bowls and one NFL Championship game (before there was a Super Bowl) over a period of four decades. Both achievements are NFL records ('64 Championship game and Super Bowl III with Baltimore; VI, VII, VIII, and XVII with Miami; and XXIX with San Diego). He received the game ball in Super Bowl VIII versus the Vikings. He is a member of the Paris (KY) High School Hall of Fame, the Miami University Hall of Fame, and the Kentucky Athletic Hall of Fame. He is the author of a book released in June 1998, titled *Arnsparger's Coaching Defensive Football,* published by CRC Press. He is co-author of the book *Football Defense of the Future,* published by Prentice-Hall, Inc. in 1998. He is also a member of Sigma Chi Fraternity—an organization that has given him two of its highest honors— a Significant Sig Medal and the Outstanding Sportsman Award in 1986.

Since retiring, Bill has been active in the Stephen Ministry program at Torry Pines Christian Church in La Jolla, CA, with the San Diego Police Department in their Volunteer in Policing program, and as a member of the Community Center Board and Architecture Review Committee in the Eastview community of Rancho Bernardo, CA. Bill and his wife, Betty Jane, have two married children, a son David and a daughter Mary Susan Klein, and two grandsons, Stephen and Christian.

JAMES A. PETERSON

Jim Peterson is a freelance writer who resides in Monterey, California with his wife, Sue. He has a BS degree in business administration from the University of California at Berkeley (1966) and an M.S. and a Ph.D. in physical education from the University of Illinois (1970, 1971). He is the author of over 50 books and more than 200 published articles on a variety of topics. Among the football books he has helped write is *Finding the Winning Edge* with Bill Walsh and Brian Billick. In 1971-1990, he served on the faculty of the United States Military Academy as a professor in the Department of Physical Education. He has appeared on several national television shows, including *CBS Evening News,* ABC's *Nightline,* and ABC's *Good Morning America.* He has long been active as a fellow in the American College of Sports Medicine and as a voluntary fund-raiser for the Make-A-Wish Foundation.